THE TASTE DIVINE

9.99

THE TASTE DIVINE

INDIAN VEGETARIAN COOKING
THE NATURAL WAY

Vanamali

STATE UNIVERSITY OF NEW YORK PRESS

The Taste Divine: Indian Vegetarian Cooking the Natural Way
by Vanamali.   State University of New York Press.
Published by State University of New York Press, Albany
© 1993 State University of New York.

Library of Congress Cataloging-in-Publication Data
10 9 8 7 6 5 4 3 2 1

Vanamali.
  The taste divine: Indian vegetarian cooking the natural way / Vanamali.
     p. cm.
  Includes index.
  ISBN 0-7914-1187-7 (ch. : acid-free). ISBN 0-7914-1188-5 (pbk.: acid-free)
  1. Cookery, Indic. 2. Cookery, Yoga. 3. Vegetarian cookery.
I. Title.
TX724.5.I4V2   1993
641.5954--dc20   92-30764
                                                                                    CIP

Design and production: Sushila Blackman, Book Packager; Tampa, Florida.

Dedicated to the Lord Vanamali.
A humble tulsi leaf laid at his Lotus feet
with love.

Contents

Introduction

In the Bhagavad Gita, Lord Krishna says, *Annath Bhavanthi Bhuthani*—"all living creatures originate from food." Since all living creatures originate from food, it is the very "stuff" of our bodies. The mind—the controlling agent of life—is strongly affected by the condition of the body. For these reasons, the spritual seeker cannot afford to ignore the effects of food on his or her state of consciousness.

As Lord Krishna rightly pointed out, a pure or sattvic diet of bland, nutritious vegetarian food not only ensures good health and longevity, but also bestows a calm and peaceful mind. The present-day world is gradually coming to realize the truth of the Lord's words pronounced nearly three thousand years ago. More and more people are coming to see that a natural vegetarian diet is conducive to a long life, and that it is better to take food "as your medicine," as Hippocrates said, than to eat in an unnatural manner and then resort to drugs to cure the resulting condition.

What Are Natural Foods?

In the Bhagavad Gita, it is said that "from the supreme being was born the extremely subtle element known as *akasa* (ether). From this came *vayu* (air), and from air came *tejas* (light) and *agni* (fire). From fire came *ap* (water). From water came *prithvi* or earth, which yielded plants. In turn, from plants, food and from food the bodies of all creatures.

Plants, it must be noted, are the effects of the interaction of the element earth with the other four elements of creation. So the virtues belonging to all five of the elements reside in food that is wholesome. Such food is considered positive, or sattvic. A live organism like the human body can only be nourished by food that is full of the qualities of life and light, not with dead carcasses. Natural hygiene prescribes fresh fruits, vegetables, and grains that have been directly exposed to the five natural energy systems or elements. They should be eaten in pure, unadulterated form—untreated and without preservatives whenever possible. When not possible, the foods should be cooked conservatively.

Food is one of the five sources of healthful living; it is also the means of curing disease. Hippocrates, the father of modern medicine, says "Let food be your medicine and medicine your food." The Bhagavad Gita classifies three types of food.

> *Sattvic foods* are bland, sweet, and agreeable. They promote long life, clear thinking, and spiritual evolution.
> *Rajasic foods* are hot, burning, pungent, sour, acrid, rough, and strong. They promote disease and aggravate the passions of the mind as well.
> *Tamasic foods* are stale, cold, impure, and rotten. They dull both body and mind, and promote disease and laziness.

As a general rule, all fruits and most vegetables and cereals are sattvic. All meat products are ruled out of this category. We need not digress into the superiority of vegetarianism over non-vegetarianism in this book, since most people who are already practicing yoga will be familiar with it.

It is not advisable to reform one's food habits all of a sudden; a gradual shift toward the ideal is preferred for those who are intent on keeping their health and prolonging their life.

Rice. Refined white rice is one of the greatest tragedies of our modern diet. For the recipes in this book, unpolished long-grain Basmati rice should be used, unless otherwise stated.

9

Dal. Dals are a good source of vegetable protein and are a must in an Indian vegetarian diet. Examples of dals include moong beans, lentils, chickpeas, pinto beans. They are more nutritive with skins.

Flour. Wholewheat flour is preferable to white flour nutritionally. For the bread recipes given in this book, it is best to use high gluten wholewheat bread flour.

For chapatis, a finely powdered wholewheat flour known as *atta* is ideal and can be found in Indian grocery stores. If this is not available, use half wholewheat flour and half unbleached white flour. This would yield nutritive chapatis, but they would not be as soft as Indian chapatis made with *atta*.

Fruits. Known as God's gift to mankind, fruits come in their own special wrappers, which make them easy to eat and handle. A proper study of man's digestive system and alimentary canal shows that nature meant man to be a fruitarian. Fruits form an important portion of any positive diet.

Vegetables. In the vegetable kingdom, leafy, green vegetables should be given pride of place, since they have imbibed the maximum qualities of sunlight, air, and ether. Tubers and root vegetables come in the second category. All vegetables, of course, should be eaten as fresh as possible, in the minimum amount of time after removal from their energy systems. It is best to choose vegetables that are organically grown, that is, grown without the aid of artificial manures and chemical fertilizers. Vegetables should be washed before peeling and cutting. They should not be washed after that. Since most of the vitamins lie just below the skin, we should eat fruits and vegetables with the skins, providing we are sure that they have not been waxed or sprayed with insecticides. The peels of organic vegetables can be saved and used to make vegetable stock for soups.

All forms of cooking reduce the food value of a vegetable, so the cooking time should be kept to a minimum. A small amount of water should be used for cooking, and this water should not be thrown away after cooking but rather used later for gravy or in soups. Ideally vegetables should be allowed to cook in their own juices, as in the case of wok cooking.

Nuts and Dried Fruits. Nuts and dried fruits form an essential part of the healthy diet, but they should not be eaten in large quantities. Considered as "condensed" food, they should be eaten sparingly. Nuts should be eaten unroasted and with their skins, except in the case of almonds. Soaking raw almonds in water overnight allows the skin to peel off easily. Tender coconut water is an excellent tonic and the milk is preferable to animal milk. The coconut is different from other nuts and contains high-quality protein. The flesh of a coconut can be used in a variety of ways, and adds both taste and nourishment to every dish. Many of the recipes in this book contain coconut in one form or another.

Milk. Milk is intended by nature for babies, but most adults all over the world consider it a necessary food item. If it is to be taken, raw milk from either a cow or a goat is preferred. If raw milk is not available, pasturized or homogenized milk can be used for the recipes in this book. In general, however, one can exist quite well taking vegetable and nut milks instead of animal milk.

Oil and Butter. Today's commercial methods of refining oils destroy many of the nutritional elements found in them. The best oils are cold pressed and unrefined, such as sunflower, sesame, and olive. The color of these oils may be darker than refined oils. Too much oil is bad for the health and so it should be used sparingly. Homemade butter is much better as a spread than margarine or ghee since it contains more water than fat. Most Indian cooking is done with unsalted ghee since cooking with butter can harm the digestive system over time. Nut butters are a good substitute for butter as a spread.

Salt. All earthly salts, if taken habitually in the slightest excess, will destroy one's health in course of time. Table salt is a highly processed food and should not be taken at all. Sea salt or rock salt (*saindav nimak*) is an alternative.

Vinegar. Natural (fruit) vinegars are generally used in Indian cooking.

Sugar. Anything sweet is assumed to be sattvic by most people, but this is far from being true. Refined sugar, whether brown or white, is a most unhealthy food and should be given up all together. It is best to use jaggery (unrefined cane sugar), which is available in most Indian grocery stores.

Honey is also called for in some recipes. It is an extremely nutritive sweetening agent with many medicinal properties, but certain qualities must be noted when using it. According to Ayurveda, the ancient Indian art of medicine, honey is a very heat-producing food. Therefore its use during hot weather should be strictly limited. Honey, when cooked, releases certain toxins that are harmful to the system. It should be added to dishes only after they have been removed from the stove and cooled a little. It can be used in winter with great benefit, since it maintains body heat. It should always be eaten with something else, never alone.

Water. One of the basic five elements of nature, water is essential for life. This does not mean, however, that we should drink gallons of water each day, as some people seem to think. Actually, if we follow a sattvic diet, most of the body's requirements for water will be met from the foods we eat. Water used for cooking and drinking should be as pure as possible. The best is rain water, but unfortunately in some places even this natural source is denied us due to atmospheric pollution. Water from springs and clean rivers, as well as water that has been exposed to sunlight, is very beneficial. Water should be drunk only when one feels thirsty. It should not be drunk before or during a meal; if necessary, a little may be taken at the end of the meal. It should be drunk very slowly, not gulped down.

Spices and Herbs. Since the taste buds play an important role in digestion, many people find it desirable to add a few spices and herbs to their meals, which enhance the taste and nutritional value of the food. Fresh green coriander (cilantro), mint, parsley, celery—and any other fresh green herb—are good for the health and can be added to any recipe. They come under the category of positive foods. Freshly grated coconut with a little lemon juice may also be added to most dishes to increase both taste and food value.

   Second to fresh green herbs come ginger, cumin, and green chilies. Other herbs—such as coriander seeds, cloves, cardamom, cinnamon, black pepper, mustard, asafoetida, aniseed, dill, caraway seeds— may be used in limited quantities. Baking soda, preservatives, and synthetic colors and flavors should be completely avoided.

Stimulants. Coffee, tea, and soda pop should also be completely avoided. They are stimulants, like alcohol and tobacco, and injure the system in course of time. We have given recipes for delicious juices and herb teas in this book, which can serve as excellent substitutes.

Yogurt, Buttermilk, Cottage Cheese. These are healthy foods, especially if they are made at home (see instructions that follow).

**Cooking Methods
& Utensils**

Methods. Cooking destroys much of the food value of vegetables. For this reason, we advise having at least one raw salad daily and using conservative cooking methods.

    Baking in a closed oven with the lid on is the best method of conserving food value.

    Steaming in a closed vessel using a little water is also good.

    Woking in a Chinese or Indian wok with no water and a tight-fitting lid—allowing the vegetables to cook in their own juices—is another fine method. A little oil can be put at the bottom of the wok.

    Boiling with a little water in a minimum amount of time—as with a pressure cooker—is also a good method.

    Frying in deep oil or ghee results in an almost complete loss of vitamins; this method should be used very sparingly. Certain rules should be followed while frying. For example, the oil should not smoke. Also, once used, oil should not be kept and reused. It is best to add salt at the end of cooking, so that the vegetables will absorb a minimum amount. Reheating of foods should be avoided.

    Sauté refers to stir frying in a little oil.

Utensils. Enamelware is one of the best kind of cooking utensil. Stainless steel may also be used. Clay pots and stoneware vessels are becoming increasingly popular and are actually the best. Aluminum should be avoided.

The pressure cooker is an invaluable asset for fast and conservative cooking. Many of the recipes given in this book make use of the pressure cooker, since it saves time and nutrients. Make sure yours is made of stainless steel, not aluminum. A pressure cooker insures that the juices are retained within the pan, which makes the food both nutritive as well as tasty. When using a pressure cooker, a few instructions need to be followed. After placing the vegetable, rice, or dal and water in the cooker, be sure that the lid is properly sealed to ensure that heat will be at its maximum. Cook at high pressure and then low pressure for a few minutes. Since pressure cookers can vary, follow the operating instructions that came with your cooker.

A *blender* is a must for those who want to have plenty of fresh juices and nut milk; it is also useful for making many of the other recipes that follow.

An *electric grinder* is also very helpful and is called for in several recipes.

A *Chinese or Indian wok* is also a great asset in the kitchen.

When to Eat. Now that we have covered what to eat, the next question is, when to eat? To eat when you are hungry and not before is a safe rule. Constant munching between meals is one of the worst crimes we make against nature. We should not eat when we are emotionally upset, as an upset mind will produce an upset stomach. A calm and quiet environment, both internally and externally, is a prerequisite for good digestion. We should not eat when we are are not well, or when we are running a temperature.

How to Eat. Eat very slowly. Solids should be drunk and liquids eaten! This sounds like a riddle, but what it means is that all solids should be masticated well, until they become semi-fluid, and then swallowed. To obtain the full nutritional value, liquids should be sipped and not gulped down.

How Much to Eat. One important thing to remember is that even sattvic foods become tamasic if taken in excess. Moderation in eating, as in everthing else, is what Lord Krishna advocates in the Bhagavad Gita. "Yoga is not for him who eats too much or for him who eats too little!" (Chapter 6, verse 16). According to the *Manu Shastra,* or code of conduct as laid down by the ancient law-giver Manu, at the end of a meal half of the stomach should be filled with food, a quarter with air, and a quarter with water.

How Many Times to Eat. Many people seem to think that four meals—breakfast, lunch, tea, and dinner—are compulsory for health. We recommend one main meal and one subsidiary one. The main meal can be taken either at lunch or dinner time, depending on your work and what is convenient with your lifestyle. Breakfast is an unnecessary evil. A glass of fruit juice can substitute well for breakfast. At tea time, a little herbal tea may be taken.

The Special Ingredient. When food is cooked with love for the Lord and served with love to His creatures, a mundane task is transformed into an evolutionary activity. Love for God overflows into love for man. There is no doubt that those who eat such food will feel the loving vibrations and benefit from them. As Lord Krishna says in the Bhagavad Gita, "Whosoever offer to me with love a flower, a leaf, a fruit, or even some water, these I will readily accept, and bless the donor of the gift." (Chapter 9, verse 26). Again He says that there is no act so menial or petty that it cannot become an offering to God.

Every act becomes charged with divinity providing it is done with love, as an offering to the divine. In the Uddhava Gita, the Lord says that all actions can be classified as sattvic, rajasic, or tamasic, but those actions that are offered to Him with love go beyond these categorizations. They are on a plane all by themselves and are known only by the *bhaktas,* or lovers of God.

Even though we may know the best type of food to eat, the right ingredients are not always available. Moreover, for those living in cities it may often be impossible to get fresh, pure, organically grown vegetables. What should one do? In these instances, we have to content ourselves with second best. However, there is a magic mantra that can transform even rajasic or tamasic food into ambrosia or *amrit*—that is the power of the Lord's name. If the food is offered to God with love before eating, then it becomes *prasad* and it cannot harm us. All its evil properties are cleansed by this act of offering. The following mantra from the Bhagavad Gita (Chapter 4, verse 24) is one that is recited when food is offered.

> *Brahmarpanam, Brahmahavi*
> *Brahmagnau, Brahmanahutham,*
> *Brahmeva thena ganthavyam*
> *Brahma karma samathina.   Aum tat sat.*

The process of eating is Brahman;
    the offering [of food] is Brahman.
The person offering is Brahman,
    and the fire is also Brahman.
Thus by seeing Brahman everywhere in action,
    he [alone] reaches Brahman.

The food offered to God purifies us. For this reason most of our recipes have been named after some aspect of Lord Krishna's divine splendor. Infinite are His forms and so Infinite are His names. Each time you make a recipe, His name will come into your mind, or perhaps some yogic qualities. Thus the mind becomes transformed even while engaged in the mundane task of cooking.

Why God in a Cookbook? We believe that there is a power inside the living body that is ever-actively safeguarding our life and health. Left to itself this power can and will cure disease, providing there is no meddling into the process by man. The purpose of food is to assist man in his evolution—physically, mentally, spiritually—and to help bring about a higher state of awareness. The same divine power that exists in man also supports and pulsates throughout the entire creation. We believe in that divine power and in the unity of all life.

Preparation of Essential Ingredients

Homemade Yogurt. Yogurt is said to have remarkable rejuvenating properties and is much better for your health than milk. Homemade yogurt is the best and is so simple to make.

4 cups raw cow's milk
2 tbs. plain yogurt, or
1 tbs. yogurt culture

Heat the milk in a pan until scalded. Do not let a skin form on the top. Keep stirring until it becomes lukewarm, or about 108°F. Pour into a glass or stoneware bowl. Add the yogurt or culture to the milk and stir until the two are completely mixed (or you could place the mixture in a blender for 1 minute). Place the bowl in a warm environment (90° to 100°F.) for 4 to 6 hours, or overnight, until it solidifies. When ready, it should fall away from the sides of the bowl, when slightly tilted. Then it should be refrigerated. This will keep for a few days. A tablespoon of yogurt from a previous batch can be used as a starter for the next batch. In cold weather, put the yogurt in a closed box with a 100 watt bulb, or in a yogurt maker.

Yogurt will only solidify if the temperature is stable. The more it is allowed to remain in the heat, the more sour it will become. For those who like their yogurt sweet, place it in the refrigerator as soon as it solidifies. If you get stuck with some sour yogurt, there is no need to throw it away; it can be used to make some of the yogurt curries or salad dressings given in this book.

Homemade Soft Cheese. Before making the cheese, make a 8" x 12" bag from a piece of cheesecloth. Fold over and stitch open end at the neck to make a space for a draw string. Put a strong plastic string through this neck.

Make yogurt with 4 cups of whole milk, as in the previous recipe. When it has solidified, pour yogurt carefully into the bag with a clean container placed below it to catch the whey. Draw the string tightly and hang up the bag, still with the container below, for about 3 to 4 hours. Shake the bag gently now and again to allow any liquid to drain. Open the bag and add any spice you like. For example, a half teaspoon of salt with either a teaspoon of aniseed or dill, or a teaspoon of caraway or celery seeds. Shake well so that the spices are well mixed. Twist the bag tightly to seal the cheese and put the bag on a plate. Place a heavy stone or iron pan over it to act as a press. Leave it in place for an hour or two, depending on how hard you

want the cheese. The more you press it, the harder the cheese becomes. When it is ready, remove from the bag and refrigerate. This
cheese can be used for sandwiches, as a filling, with salads, or
sprinkled on top of tostadas, pizzas, or any dish that calls for cheese.

Since this cheese is made without rennet, it is ideal for vegetarians.
The whey is very nutritious and can be used in curries and soups. It
can also be given to invalids and those with upset stomachs.

Paneer. Also called Indian Cottage Cheese, paneer keeps easily for a
week refrigerated. Before using in curries, it should be lightly fried.

> 4 cups whole milk
> 4 tbs. strained lemon juice
> cheesecloth bag or large, clean handkerchief

Bring the milk to a boil, stirring occasionally to stop a skin from
forming. Lower heat and add lemon juice. Stir gently until all the milk
has separated into curds and whey. The whey should be clear; if not,
add a little more lemon juice. Remove from the heat and pour into a
cheesecloth bag or colander lined with a handkerchief. Place a container below to catch the whey, which will strain very quickly. Twist
the cloth to seal the cheese and put it on a plate. Put a heavy stone or
iron pot over it for an hour. The paneer will be quite hard. Rinse
cheese in water, cut into cubes, and refrigerate. It will easily keep for
a week.

Homemade Butter. In India, butter is traditionally made from yogurt,
not from cream. The liquid left over after churning the butter is
buttermilk. Thus, by this method, one gets both butter and buttermilk
from yogurt. Make yogurt with 4 cups of whole milk, as in the

20

recipe given earlier. When the yogurt has solidifed, pour it in a blender, add a cup of cold water, and blend at slow speed until it separates into butter and buttermilk. Large lumps of butter will start forming around the sides of the blender. Pour liquid into a bowl, remove the butter with a spoon, and place it in a bowl of water. It does not need to be salted. This homemade treat will keep refrigerated for a week and can be used in any recipes that call for butter.

Buttermilk makes an excellent health drink, either plain or flavored. It is non-fatty and low in cholesterol. Buttermilk is highly recommended, even in cases of diarrhea, dysentry, or fever.

Homemade Ghee. Ghee, or clarified butter, is often used in Indian cooking. Although it keeps much longer than butter, ghee is a very rich food and should be used sparingly. Ghee is better to cook with than butter since butter leaves a residue when heated that, in the long run, will harm the system. This toxic residue has already been removed from ghee. Butter should not be heated but rather added to the food after it has been cooked and removed from the heat.

Make butter, as specified in the previous recipe, and place the butter in a heavy saucepan. Cook over medium heat, stirring occasionally until the butter starts to boil. When the surface is covered with a frothy white foam, turn the heat down low.

Simmer uncovered, stirring ocassionally until gelatinous solids have formed on the surface. Remove from the heat immediately. The ideal color of ghee is a clear pale gold. It becomes dark when it is cooked too long and the residue from the butter starts to burn. Remove the clear liquid with a ladle without disturbing the bottom of the pan. Pour it through a piece of cheesecloth or handkerchief arranged over a jar. Cool this ghee to room temperature before covering. For storage, ghee does not need to be refrigerated. Seal it with a tightly closed lid and place in a cool place for a month or more. The dregs can be strained and used to sauté onions or vegetables for curries. The solid material can be thrown away, since it contains toxic matter.

How to Sprout Pulses & Cereals

Pulses is a generic term for dried seeds of beans, lentils and peas. Sprouting pulses, such as lentils, in your own kitchen is a simple process. Sprouts are a food source brimming with life and energy. They are among the richest protein foods in the vegetable kingdom. Best eaten raw in salads or any other dish, they can also be lightly steamed. A sprouter can be found in health food stores or a plain jar may be used.

Grains can be sprouted, dried and powdered, and used as flour; when this is done, the resulting flour is a type of malt that has a high food value. We recommend eating some type of sprout daily. Almost all pulses and grains can be sprouted, providing their skins are intact. Moong dal is one of the easiest and most nutritious to sprout.

1 cup moong beans	cheesecloth bag
2 cups water	

Soak the beans overnight in water. In the morning drain off the water and rinse well. Tie up the soaked beans in a cheesecloth bag and hang it in a dark place. In the evening rinse once again and hang overnight as before. Rinse and drain morning and evening for three days, until the sprouts are well formed. Wash off the excess hull before using. Sprouts are best when used immediately, but they can be kept in a plastic container in the refrigerator for a few days.

How to Make Garam Masala

Garam Masala is a special blend of spices that is commonly used in Indian cooking. It not only adds flavor to the food but helps to preserve it, since many of these spices have disinfectant properties.

1 tbs. black cardamom seeds
2 tbs. cinnamon bark
2 tbs. dill seeds

2 tbs. cloves
2 tbs. black peppercorns
2 tsp. bay leaves

Dry all ingredients very well and grind into a fine powder with an electric grinder. Keep in an air-tight container. This mixture can be used in all recipes calling for garam masala.

One should become a sabhari kanua (one who, having conserved his vitality by proper eating, has gained wisdom) to become closer to the Lord. Thus becoming wise, one eats to live and does not live to eat.

—SAMA VEDA

Chapter One:
Sadhana
Juices & Shakes

Fresh vegetable and fruit juices are a source of constant joy and should be substituted for tea and coffee as breakfast drinks. All fruits and most vegetables make excellent juices. A few unusual combinations are given below. We suggest diluting the juices slightly with water. They should be drunk very slowly, with no additional salt. Tender coconut water is the best of all health drinks. Since nut milks and yogurt shakes are also good substitute breakfast drinks, they are included in this section. The following recipes will each make about two 8-ounce glasses of juice.

1. Archana/Vegetable Juice (Serves 2)

1 large carrot

1 stalk celery or coriander

2 cups water

1 beetroot

1/2" piece of ginger

1 tomato

Clean and chop vegetables and herbs coarsley. Put them through a juicer or blender and strain; serve immediately.

2. Pooja/Tomato Juice (Serves 2)

1 cup chopped tomatoes

1 cup water

1 bunch fresh coriander leaves,
   chopped

a dash of pepper

2 tbs. honey

Put tomatoes and coriander through a blender. Strain, add honey and a dash of pepper, and serve.

3. Aradhana/Lemon-Mint Juice (Serves 2)

1 large lemon

1 tbs. honey

1" piece of fresh ginger

1 small bunch fresh mint
   leaves

2 cups boiling water

Combine squeezed lemon juice and extracted ginger juice. To juice ginger, grate it in a small, fine grater or put it through a blender with a little water. Pour boiling water over mint leaves and allow to cool. Strain leaves, mix with juices and honey, and chill. Serve with a sprig of mint.

4. Samyama/Cucumber Juice (Serves 2)

1 large cucumber
1 stalk of celery or coriander
   leaves
1 tomato
1 cup water

Clean and chop vegetables and herbs coarsely and put ingredients through blender. Strain, and serve immediately.

5. Niyama/Green Juice (Serves 2)

1 head lettuce
1 cucumber
1 bunch mint, coriander, or stalk
   of celery
4 green beans
1/2 tsp. chopped jalapeno
1 cup water
1/2 cup sprouts (any kind)

Clean and chop vegetables coarsely and put them through a blender. Strain, and serve immediately.

6. Asana/Orange Juice (Serves 2)

3 tbs. fresh peppermint leaves
2 orange slices
juice of 2 oranges
2 tbs. honey
2 cups water

Boil water and pour over peppermint leaves. Cool liquid and strain. Add orange juice and heat, but do not boil. Remove from heat and add honey. Serve hot with a few slices of orange.

7. Yoga/Fruit Juice (Serves 2)

1 apple	1 orange
1/2 cup pineapple	1 cup water

Clean and chop fruits coarsely and put them through a blender with water. Strain, and serve immediately.

8. Pranayama/Banana Shake (Serves 2)

2 tbs. almonds	1 banana, chopped
1 tsp. honey	1 cup water

Place water in the blender and turn it on. Drop the almonds in while the machine is running and blend for 3 minutes. Add banana and honey and blend. Serve immediately.

9. Dharana/Cashew Milk (Serves 2)

1/4 cup cashew nuts, raw	1/2 tsp. honey
1 drop vanilla extract	2 cups water

Grind cashew in an electric grinder until powdered. Put all ingredients except vanilla in a blender and blend at high speed. Add vanilla and serve immediately.

10. Japa/Mixed-Fruit Shake (Serves 3)

1 cup cubed papaya	1 banana, chopped
1/2 cup apple juice	1/2 cup cold water

Put all ingredients through a blender until smooth. Serve immediately.

11. Dhyana/Carrot Juice (Serves 1)

1 cup chopped carrots	1/2 tsp. honey
1/2 cup coconut milk	

Put ingredients through a blender, strain, and serve. (Although coconut milk is preferred, cow's milk may be substituted if necessary. The method for making coconut milk is given in Chapter 3.)

12. Brahmacharya/Papaya Milk (Serves 1)

1 cup chopped papaya
1/2 cup coconut milk
1 tsp. honey

Put ingredients through a blender and serve immediately. Fruit nectars can be made in this way with any pulpy fruit like bananas, papayas, cheekoo, peaches, and mangoes.

13. Dhriti/Mango Shake (Serves 2)

1/2 cup yogurt
1 tsp. honey
1 mango
1 cup water

Remove the pulp from the mango. Put all ingredients through a blender, chill, and serve.

14. Tapas/Sour Buttermilk (Serves 1)

1 cup buttermilk
1 tsp. honey
1 tsp. lemon juice
1/2 tsp. ginger juice
1/4 tsp. jalapenos, finely
 chopped
a pinch of salt

Blend all ingredients in a blender at high speed and serve frothing.

15. Samadhi/Sweet Buttermilk (Serves 1)

1 glass buttermilk
1 tsp. honey
1/4 tsp. lemon juice

Blend all ingredients in blender and serve immediately.

Chapter Two:
Gokul
Herbal Teas

The black tea drinking habit is a real curse of modern civilization. Our forefathers did not have this habit. Instead they made teas or tisanes from fresh herbs; their lives were healthier than ours, despite the advantages of our modern technology. The cost of making herbal teas is negligible. In every garden we can find a flavor to suit our taste. Thus these herbs are both palatable and, since they are high in vitamins, nutritious. Cloves are highly antiseptic and because of this they are used in curries. In many temples cloves are added to the consecrated water that is given to the pilgrims. Although many gardeners hate the dandelion, its medicinal properties are very great. Almost all parts of this herb are good. The young leaves are tasty in salads and sandwiches. A decoction made from the roots is excellent for liver disorders. At Vanamali, we have a favorite decoction that we call Holy Herbal Tea. It is made from the holy plant Tulsi, or Holy Basil, which was Krishna's favorite.

Decocotion Extraction of essence by boiling 3 minutes and straining

Infusion To steep in boiling water and allow to remain for 5 minutes before straining

Catarrhal Pertaining to inflammation of the mucous membrane of the nose and throat.

Carminative Able to cure flatulence.

Each of the recipes that follow will yield two 8-ounce cups of tea.

16. Tulsi /Holy Basil Tea

1 tbs. fresh or 1/2 tbs. dried
   tulsi seeds and leaves
1 tbs. fresh or 1/4 tbs. dried
   orange peel
1 tsp. honey
2 cups water

Boil the tulsi and orange peel in the water, and allow mixture to stand for 5 minutes. Strain, add honey, and serve either hot or cold.

17. Abhaya/Ginger-Mint Tea

1 tsp. fresh ginger, grated
2 tsp. honey
2 cups boiling water
a few fresh mint leaves

Pour boiling water over the ginger and mint and allow to stand for 5 minutes. Strain and add honey. Drink either hot or cold.

18. Acharya/Aniseed Tea

Aniseed is an ancient remedy that was used by the Greeks, Romans, Egyptians, and Hindus for overcoming digestive disorders. Even to this day, most East Indians eat a little aniseed after a meal.

2 tsp. aniseed
1 tsp. honey
2 tsp. fresh peppermint leaves
2 cups boiling water

Infuse the aniseed and peppermint in boiling water. Strain and add honey. Take before bedtime to help cure a cold or to improve digestion.

19. Ahimsa/Clove Tea

2 cloves
2 cups boiling water
honey to taste (optional)

Pour boiling water over the cloves and allow to stand for 10 minutes. May be taken with or without honey, either hot or cold.

20. Akshara/Dandelion Tea

5 dandelion flowers
2 cups water

1 tsp. honey

Boil water and infuse the flowers. Allow to stand for 3 minutes. Strain, add honey, and serve.

21. Akasha/Lime Flower Tea

2 tsp. fresh lime flowers
1 tsp. honey

2 cups boiling water

Boil water and infuse the flowers in it. Allow to stand for 10 minutes. Strain, add honey, and take at teatime. This drink is good for catarrhal conditions and nervous headaches.

22. Ananda/Mint Tea

Mint is a carminative. The whole plant, either fresh or dried, can be made into tea by the addition of boiling water. It stops vomiting, soothes a disordered stomach, and improves the appetite. Mint tea can be taken with a slice of lemon and sweetened with honey. Adding a little ground fresh ginger increases the flavor.

2 tbs. fresh mint leaves
1 tsp. grated fresh ginger

2 cups boiling water
honey to taste

Pour boiling water over the mint leaves and ginger, and allow to stand for 5 minutes. Strain and add honey. Serve hot or cold with a sprig of fresh mint.

23. Avatara/Peppermint Tea

Peppermint tea is one of the safest and most pleasant tasting antiseptics. It arrests the spread of tubercle, relieves coughs, assists nutrition, and helps to increase weight. The addition of peppermint leaves to any other tea improves its flavor. Like ordinary mint, it can be grown in any garden.

2 tbs. fresh peppermint leaves   honey to taste
2 cups boiling water

Pour boiling water over the peppermint leaves, and allow to stand for 5 minutes. Strain and serve hot or cold with honey.

24. Avikarya/Rose Tea
While rose is a very popular fragrance and the rose flower is lovely, few people in the West realize its medicinal properties. Rose petal tea strengthens the heart and is good for the liver. It soothes the mucous linings of the body and helps cure coughs. A mild rose solution is excellent for cleansing the eyes.

2 tbs. fresh rose petals (preferably   2 cups boiling water
    fragrant) or, 1 tbs. dried
    (fragrant) rose petals

Pour boiling water over rose petals and allow to stand for 5 minutes. Strain and add honey.

25. Avyakta/Saffron Tea
The excellent medicinal properties of saffron have long been recognized in the East but its exorbitant cost places it out of the reach of most people. With a distinct flavor, this tea is a brain stimulant and also strengthens the sight and hearing.

small pinch of saffron powder   2 cups boiling water

Pour boiling water over the saffron powder. Stir until it dissolves. Allow to stand for 3 minutes before drinking.

O iniquitous soul, you do not give me—your stomach—even twenty-four minutes of rest throughout the day; not ever are you aware of the great suffering you inflict on me at all times. Understand that hereafter I cannot bear to live with you.

—RAMANA MAHARSHI

Chapter Three: Balakrishna Milks, Butter & Cream

26. Atma/Ginger Tonic
The following recipe will make about six quart-sized bottles of ginger tonic. A little of this may be put into a glass and cold water may be added. This is a refreshing drink in hot weather.

1/2 cup fresh ginger
8 cups jaggery
2 tbs. honey

juice of 2 lemons
5 quarts water

Crush the ginger with an electric grinder or mortar and pestle. Put ginger in a large saucepan with a quart of water. Bring to a boil and then simmer for 1/2 an hour. Place the sugar, lemon juice, and honey in a bowl. Pour this mixture into the ginger water and stir well. Boil the remaining water and add to the ginger water. Stir well and cover for 24 hours. Strain and bottle. If bottles are corked and kept in a cool place, this tonic will keep for about 2 weeks at the most.

Balakrishna, or Baby Krishna, loved milk, butter, and cream. And since he lived in a cowherd settlement, these dairy products were all freshly made. In the modern age, we are forced to depend on processed dairy products. For a special treat, try the following recipes and enjoy these products fresh, as he did.

One glass in any of the recipes that follow refers to an 8-ounce glass, or one cup.

27. Bhakti/Coconut Milk (4 Cups)
1 cup freshly grated coconut   4 cups boiling water

Combine the grated coconut with 2 cups of the boiling water and mix in a blender for a few minutes. Let mixture stand until the water cools, then strain. The residue may be soaked in the remaining 2 cups of boiling water, allowed to stand for 15 minutes, then strained. This thin "second" milk (2 cups) may be used as a substitute for water in curries, soup, and stews. The first milk (2 cups) can be used for desserts and drinks and for curries that call for thick milk. (The remaining pulp may be composted.)

28. Bharta/Cashew Milk (2 Cups)

1/2 cup cashews   2 cups water

Grind the cashews in an electric grinder into a fine meal. Add water and honey and put through a blender for 2 minutes. Use immediately; if allowed to stand, blend again just before using.

All types of nut milk may be made in this way.

29. Bansali/Sesame Milk (2 Glasses)

1/2 cup sesame seeds   1/4 tsp. vanilla extract
2 cups water

Grind the unroasted sesame seeds into a fine powder. Put all ingredients through a blender at high speed for 2 minutes. Pour mixture through a fine strainer and discard the meal. The milk can be used in soups, gravies, and puddings.

30. Brindavan/Soya Bean Milk (8 Glasses)

1-1/2 cups soya beans   11 cups water

Clean and wash the beans and place in a glass or steel bowl. Add 4-1/2 cups cold water and cover overnight. The next day, grind the beans in an electric blender for 2 minutes, with the same water in which they have been soaked.

Boil 6 1/2 cups of water in a large pan and add the blended bean mixture. Boil for 8 minutes on low heat. Keep stirring frequently with a wooden spoon. Meanwhile line a colander with two layers of cheesecloth. Place the colander in a pan large enough to hold all the milk that is heating. Pour the milk into the colander and let it drain. Gather the four ends of the cloth and squeeze out the remaining milk.

This milk can be used in most recipes calling for cow's milk. It can also be drunk instead of cow's milk. Like fresh cow's milk, fresh soy milk lasts only a few days in the refrigerator. Remember that soya milk is a very high protein food (higher in protein than meat), so it should be used sparingly.

The pulp may be put into soups or baked dishes, or, combined with boiled potatoes and garam masala and made into patties. While it does not have much food value, the pulp can provide roughage.

31. Brahman/Nut Cream (1 Cup)

1 tbs. raw cashew nuts	1 tbs. coconut milk (see p. 32)
1 tbs. raw almonds	1/4 tsp. vanilla extract
1 tbs. honey	1/2 cup water

Grind the nuts into a fine powder. Put through a blender with water until well combined. Strain through a fine mesh and remove the pulp, which may be used in breads or puddings. Return the creamy liquid to a blender. Add the coconut milk, honey, and vanilla, and blend until smooth. Nut cream can be made from all nuts in this way. It can be used in fruit salads and desserts in place of regular cream.

Having become the Vaishwanara fire [fire of digestion], it is I who abide in all living beings, and having united with Prana and Apana, it is I who digest the four types of food.

—BHAGAVAD GITA,
CHAPTER 15, VERSE 14

32. Bhajan/Peanut Butter (1 Cup)

1 cup peanuts, with skins
1/4 cup water
1/8 cup peanut oil
honey to taste

Dry the peanuts well in the sun or roast them in the oven before grinding or they will cling to the grinder. Grind in a electric grinder into a fine meal. Add the honey, water, and peanut oil. Mix together well, either by hand or with a blender until the desired consistency is reached. In a closed jar, this peanut butter will keep refrigerated for a couple of weeks. Butter from other nuts can be made in the same way.

Although Western style salads are not traditional in India, raitas and chutneys are very popular. Raita refers to fresh vegetables or fruits mixed in yogurt with a masala; chutney refers to vegetables and/or coconut ground with chilies and other masalas.

33. Deva/Cucumber Raita (Serves 2)

2 cucumbers, grated
1 cup fresh yogurt
1/2 tsp. black pepper powder
1/2 tsp. cumin powder
1/2 tsp. salt
2 tbs. chopped coriander leaves

Cumin powder that is to be used in salads should be roasted and powdered. To make an ample supply, dry roast 1/2 cup of cumin seeds in a frying pan without oil until they turn dark brown. Grind seeds into a fine powder and store in an airtight bottle.

In a bowl, mix yogurt, salt, pepper, and cucumber. Add coriander leaves. Sprinkle 1/2 teaspoon of cumin powder on top and mix just before serving.

Chapter Four: Damodara Salads

Boiled or mashed potatoes, or fresh bananas, may be used instead of cucumbers in this recipe.

34. Dharma/Beetroot Raita (Serves 2)

1 large beetroot, grated
2 cups yogurt, well-beaten
1 small jalapeno chili, chopped
1/2 cup coconut, grated

1 tsp. black mustard seeds
1 tsp. salt
2 tbs. coriander leaves

Grind the coconut, mustard seeds, and green chili and add to the yogurt. Add salt and combine mixture with the beetroot. Top with coriander leaves.

35. Advaita/Tomato Raita (Serves 2)

2 tomatoes
1/2 cup grated coconut
1 cucumber
2 cups yogurt, beaten
1 jalapeno, chopped

1 tsp. black mustard seeds
1 tsp. salt
1/2 tsp. honey
2 tbs. chopped coriander leaves

Grind coconut, mustard seeds, and green chili. Combine with the yogurt, along with the salt and honey. Chop the tomatoes and cucumber into fairly small pieces and add to the yogurt mixture. Garnish with coriander leaves.

36. Dhira/Eggplant Chutney (Serves 2)

1 large eggplant *(brinjal)*
2 tbs. chopped coriander leaves
2 tbs. each oil and lemon juice
1 tsp. honey
2 tsp. grated ginger

1 jalapeno chili, minced
1 tsp. salt
lettuce leaves and tomato slices
a few pinches of roasted cumin
    powder

Coat eggplant with oil. Prick with fork and roast over hot coals or in the oven until tender. When cool, remove the skin and mash flesh well. Add remaining ingredients and mix well. Serve on individual lettuce leaves, surrounded by tomato slices. Sprinkle with roasted cumin powder and serve chilled.

Variation: Mix in 1 cup of yogurt before adding cumin.

37. Dwaraka/Mixed Vegetable Salad (Serves 2)

2 cups small cauliflower pieces
1/2 cup finely chopped tomatoes
1 tbs. minced onion
2 tbs. chopped coriander leaves
1 jalapeno chili, minced
1 tbs. lemon juice
1 cup lightly roasted peanuts, coarsely ground
1/2 tsp. salt
1/2 tsp. honey

Toss all ingredients in a salad bowl and serve immediately.

38. Devaki/Mixed Vegetable Salad (Serves 4)

2 cups grated carrot
1 cup minced cabbage
1 cup small cauliflower pieces
1 cup grated turnip
1/2 cup freshly grated coconut
2 tbs. chopped coriander leaves
2 tbs. lemon juice
1 tsp. honey
1/2 tsp. salt
1/2 tsp. black pepper powder
a few lettuce leaves

Mix lemon juice, salt, pepper, and honey together in a large bowl and toss in the vegetables. Arrange vegetables on individual lettuce leaves and top with grated coconut. Serve immediately.

Joy, temperence, and repose slam the door on the doctor's nose.

— H.W. LONGFELLOW

39. Daruka/Carrot-Cheese Salad (Serves 4)

2 cups grated carrots
1 cup soft paneer (see p. 20)
2 tbs. chopped coriander leaves
2 large tomatoes, cut into wedges

1 tsp. black pepper powder
1/2 tsp. salt
a few tender cabbage or lettuce leaves

Mix the grated carrot and coriander leaves with pepper and salt. Place a dollup of this mixture on individual lettuce or cabbage leaves and top with cottage cheese. Place a few tomato wedges on side of dish and serve.

40. Draupadi/Fruit-Nut Salad (Serves 4)

1 cup grated carrot
1/2 cup shredded cabbage
1/4 cup raisins
1/4 cup chopped walnuts

1/2 cup diced apples
1 tbs. grated orange rind
1 orange, peeled and segmented
1 tsp. roasted cumin powder

Toss vegetables, fruit, and nuts together and place on a platter. Sprinkle with cumin powder and arrange orange segments around the edge of platter. (Sesame salt can be used instead of cumin powder. To make sesame salt, dry roast sesame seeds in a frying pan until lightly browned. Add salt and put through electric grinder. Keep sesame salt in an air-tight bottle and use for salads, just like cumin powder.)

41. Vasudeva/Fruit Salad (Serves 2)

2 ripe avocados, chopped
1 apple, chopped
1 orange, peeled and segmented

1 cup moong sprouts
1/4 cup orange juice
1/2 tsp. honey

Mix all ingredients together and serve immediately.

42. Yashoda/Sprout Salad (Serves 4)

1 cup moong bean sprouts
1/2 cup peanut sprouts
1/4 cup grated coconut
1/4 tsp. grated ginger

2 tbs. chopped coriander leaves
1 carrot, grated
2 tbs. mayonnaise (see p. 41)

Toss all ingredients together and serve immediately.

43. Nanda/Green Salad (Serves 4)

2 cups of greens (spinach, lettuce,
     or cabbage leaves)
1/4 cup moong sprouts
1/4 cup wheat sprouts

2 ripe tomatoes, cut in rounds
1 carrot, cut in rounds
2 tbs. nut-cream dressing (see p. 34)

Mix the greens, sprouts, and dressing together. Arrange on a platter
with tomato and carrot rounds.

44. Subhadra/Mixed Salad (Serves 4)

2 cups shredded cabbage
1 cup chopped apples
1/4 cup chopped walnuts

1 cup chopped celery
1/4 cup raisins
1/4 cup mayonaise (see p. 41)

Toss all ingredients in mayonnaise and serve.

45. Kuchela/Cucumber-Boat Salad (Serves 4)

2 large cucumbers
2 tbs. chopped mint leaves
1 tbs. chopped onion

1 large tomato, chopped
2 tbs. mayonnaise (see p. 41)
1/2 cup soft cheese (see p. 19)

Slice the cucumbers in half lengthwise. Scoop out and chop the insides.
Add all remaining ingredients, except the cheese, to the cucumber mix.

Drain off excess water and scoop the mixture back into the cucumber boats. Sprinkle with cheese and garnish with mint leaves. Chill slightly before serving.

46. Arjuna/Mixed Salad (Serves 4)

1 large cucumber	1/4 cup chopped cashews
1 large tomato, sliced	1 carrot, chopped
1/4 cup chopped almonds	1/2 cup sour cream

Peel the cucumber and press a fork along its sides to make a design, then cut into rounds. Mix all ingredients together and serve.

47. Yadava/BeetRoot Salad (Serves 2)

1 cup grated beetroot	2 tsp. sesame salt
1 cup grated radish, white or red	several cabbage or lettuce
1/4 cup freshly grated coconut	leaves

Arrange a bed of lettuce leaves on a platter. Sprinkle with sesame salt. Now arrange the grated beets and radish in alternate layers to form a wheel pattern. First the radish on the outside of the wheel, then the beets. Place the grated coconut in the hub of the wheel and serve.

48. Balarama/Tomato Bites (Serves 4)

4 small tomatoes	4 tbs. chopped coriander leaves
4 tbs. finely chopped spinach	1/2 tsp. salt
4 tbs. grated coconut	1/2 tsp. black pepper powder

Cut three vertical slits in each tomato, very carefully so as not to spoil its shape. In the first opening, stuff a little spinach, in the next a little coconut, and in the third a little coriander leaves. Sprinkle with salt and pepper and serve.

Man may be superior or inferior, according to the food eaten ....

— Mahatma Gandhi

Salad dressings and sauces are not a part of traditional Indian cooking. However, lately they have become popular with the increasing interest in salads. They add zest to a plain salad and bring their own nutritive value.

49. Radha/Tomato Sauce (About 1-1/4 quarts)

1 lb. chopped tomato
1/2 cup jaggery
2 tsp. salt
1 large onion, chopped
1" piece fresh ginger, chopped
1 tsp. red chili powder

1 tsp. fresh cumin powder
1/2 tsp. cardamom powder
1 tsp. cinnamon powder
4 cloves, powdered
1/4 tsp. mace powder*

Blend all ingredients in blender without adding water. Cook in heavy bottomed pan for 1/2 an hour or until a fairly thick sauce is obtained. This sauce can be cooled, bottled, and kept in the refrigerator for a month.
* Ground mace is available at Indian and Middle Eastern groceries.

50. Rukmani/Mayonnaise (1 Cup)

3 tbs. raw cashews
1/2 cup water
1/2 tbs. natural vinegar
1/2 tsp. salt
1 tbs. lemon juice

1 tbs. honey
1 tsp. yellow mustard powder
1/2 tsp. black pepper powder
1/4-1/2 cup oil

Place cashews and water in blender and grind for a minute. Add salt, lemon juice, vinegar, honey, mustard, and pepper and blend well. Without turning off the blender, add a drop of oil at a time until the mixture thickens. Bottle and keep in the refrigerator for a month. This dressing tastes just like mayonnaise.

Overeating leads to progressive deterioration of health. It reduces the span of life. It is heaven-closing. It is vice-oriented. The glutton is disliked by all the people around. Hence give up over eating.

— THE LAWS OF MANU

51. Sathyabhama/Lemon Dressing (1/2 Cup)

2 tbs. oil   pinch of salt
2 tbs. honey   dash of black pepper
2 tbs. lemon juice

Mix well with a hand beater or in a blender. This plain salad dressing can be used for any salad. It also may be mixed with any nut cream.

52. Jambhavathi/Banana Dressing (1 Cup)

2 large ripe bananas   1 tbs. honey
2 tbs. nut cream (cashew or almond)   1 tbs. lemon juice

Mash bananas. Add remaining ingredients and blend. This dressing goes well with all fruit salads.

53. Mitrabinda/Citrus Dressing (1/2 Cup)

2 tbs. orange or grapefruit juice   2 tbs. apple or pineapple juice
2 tbs. lemon juice   1 tbs. honey

Blend together and serve over fruits.

54. Sathya/Orange Dressing (1/4 Cup)

juice of one large orange   1 tbs. honey
1 tbs. almond butter

Mix almond butter and honey together. Then slowly add the juice and blend until a smooth cream is obtained. This makes a good topping for fruit salads.

55. Kalindi/Cheese Dressing (1 Cup)

1 cup soft cheese (see p. 19)   1/2 tsp. each black pepper and salt
1 tbs. lemon juice   2 tbs. honey

Whip cheese and honey until thick. Add pepper and salt, then slowly mix in lemon juice.

56. Lakshmana/Chinese Dressing (1/4 Cup)

4 tbs. soya sauce
2 tsp. natural vinegar
1/4 cup grated carrot

Blend all ingredients well. This sauce will go well with Chinese dishes.

57. Bhadra/Carrot Dressing (1/2 Cup)

1/4 cup grated carrot
1/4 cup oil
1 tbs. natural vinegar
1/2 tsp. black pepper powder

Blend all ingredients until well mixed. This dressing can be used on all vegetable salads.

Chapter Six: Shyamasundara Soups

Soups are nourishing, filling, and easy to make—especially if you have a pressure cooker. The old fashioned way of making soups is to cook them for hours so as to extract all the nourishment from the ingredients. From our point of view, the less you cook vegetables the better. So these soups can be made very fast.

Most people tend to throw away the most nutritious part of any vegetable — the skin. Since all vitamins are found immediately beneath the skin, it is a great pity if they are wasted. However, if vegetables are grown using chemical manures and sprays, it would not be advisable to use the skin. If you can get organically grown vegetables, the skins should be kept to make stock, which can be used later as a base for soups or gravies.

To Make Stock From Vegetable Peelings

Wash the vegetable well before cutting (never wash vegetables after cutting). Collect the seeds, peelings, and any other part not used in actual cooking. To one cup of vegetable peelings add 3 cups of water and boil in a pressure cooker. Cook for 3 minutes after bringing to maximum pressure. When cool, mash well and strain.

The following recipes make 2 to 3 servings, unless otherwise marked. See note on pressure cooking, page 15.

58. Guru/Lentil Soup

1 cup lentils or any dal, preferably with skin
1 tbs. ghee
3 cups water
1 onion, chopped
1 carrot, sliced

3 tomatoes, chopped
1 tsp. fresh cumin powder
1/2 tsp. black pepper powder
salt to taste
lemon juice to taste

Wash lentils and boil with water in pressure cooker for 4 minutes after full pressure is reached. Open the cooker as soon as possible and add the tomatoes, carrot, and 3/4 of the onion. Replace lid to retain flavors and allow to cool, then blend all ingredients together. In a separate pan, heat ghee and sauté remaining onion. When onion is soft, add cumin, pepper, and salt. Pour into the lentil mixture. If it is too thick, add a little water. Serve hot with a few drops of lemon juice.

59. Gita/Spinach Soup

3 cups fresh spinach
1 tsp. chopped onions
1 tbs. ghee
1/2 tsp. black pepper powder

1 tsp. salt
1 cup water
1/4 cup nut or soya milk (optional)

Lightly boil spinach in 1 cup of water and put through a blender. Heat ghee and sauté the onions. Add blended spinach and salt and pepper. Nut or soya milk may be mixed in if desired.

60. Gopala/Cauliflower Soup

1 medium-sized cauliflower, chopped (broccoli or cabbage may be used instead)
1/2 onion, chopped
1/2 cup raw cashews
1 tsp. fresh butter
1 tsp. sweet basil
1 tsp. salt
1/2 tsp. black pepper powder
2 cups water
1/4 cup vegetable stock

Put cauliflower and onion in a pressure cooker with water. Cook for 1 minute after bringing to maximum pressure. Open immediately to release steam. With a small amount of vegetable stock, make a nut cream with the cashews. Put the vegetables through a blender, transfer to a pan, and cook over low heat for 3 minutes. Add basil, salt, and pepper. Slowly add the nut cream and mix well. Cook on low heat for 1 minute. Add butter and serve.

61. Giridhara/Tomato Soup

5 large tomatoes, chopped
1 small onion, chopped
1 stalk celery, chopped
1 cup water
2 tbs. ghee
1/2 cup thick coconut milk (see p. 32)
2 tbs. sweet basil
1 tsp. honey
pepper and salt to taste

Blend tomatoes with water and strain. Heat ghee and sauté onion and celery. Add tomato juice and cook for 2 minutes. Put this mixture, with strained tomatoes, through a blender then return to the pan and add salt, pepper, and basil. Slowly add the coconut milk and heat, but do not boil. Add honey after removing from heat.

62. Govinda/Spicy Tomato Soup

5 large ripe tomatoes, chopped
2 tbs. chopped coriander leaves
1 onion, minced
1 tsp. grated ginger
1 tbs. sweeet basil leaves

2 tbs. ghee
3 cups stock or water
1 tbs. honey
salt and pepper to taste

Heat the ghee and sauté 1 tablespoon of the minced onion in it. Put remaining ingredients through a blender and strain. Add blended tomato mixture to the sautéed onions and cook for 3 minutes. Add salt and pepper, and mix well. Add honey after removing from heat.

63. Gopi/Lentil-Beetroot Soup

1/2 cup lentils or any dal
1 beetroot, chopped
4 cups water or stock
1 tbs. fresh mint
1 tsp. freshly grated ginger

1 tbs. lemon juice or 1/4 cup
    yogurt
2 tbs. ghee
2 tbs. chopped onion
salt and pepper to taste

Put the beetroot, lentils, and ginger with water in a pressure cooker. Cook for 5 minutes after bringing to maximum pressure. Cool and blend. In a separate pan, sauté onions in ghee; add the blended soup, salt, pepper, and yogurt or lemon. Mix thoroughly and serve hot. Sprinkle fresh mint on top.

64. Hrishikesha/Potato Soup (Serves 4 or 5)

4 potatoes, diced with skins
4 cups water
1/2 onion, minced
1/2 onion, chopped
1 stalk celery, chopped

1/2 cup coconut milk
2 tbs. ghee
1 tsp. chopped parsley
salt and pepper to taste

Put the potatoes and chopped onion with water in pressure cooker. Cook for 4 minutes after bringing to maximum pressure. Cool, peel skin, and put through a blender. In a separate pan, sauté the minced onion in ghee. Add celery and sauté. Add potato mixture, salt, and pepper. Slowly add coconut milk and heat, but do not boil. Serve with chopped parsley.

65. Govardhan/Mixed Vegetable Soup (Serves 4)

2 tomatoes, chopped	2 bay leaves
1 large potato, diced	1/2 tsp. sweet basil
1 large carrot, diced	1/2 tsp. black pepper powder
1/2 cup green beans, chopped	1 small piece ginger, chopped
1/2 cup green peas	1 onion, chopped
1 large turnip, chopped	4 cups water
1/4 cup chopped cauliflower pieces	salt and butter to taste
1/4 cup shredded cabbage	1/2 cup fresh coconut milk
2 celery stalks, sliced	(optional, for creamy soup)

Put the tomatoes and 2 cups of water through a blender and strain. Place remaining ingredients, along with the blended tomato, in the pressure cooker. Cook for 3 minutes after full pressure is reached. Add a small amount of fresh butter and serve hot.

To make into a creamy soup, don't blend tomatoes separately but cook them instead in the pressure cooker with other vegetables. When cooked, put all ingredients through the blender. Then return mixture to the pressure cooker and add 1/2 cup fresh coconut milk. Mix thoroughly but do not boil.

66. Hari/Carrot Soup

4 carrots, diced
1 medium-sized onion, chopped
1/2 cup coconut milk
1 stalk celery, chopped

1 tbs. ghee
3 cups water
salt and pepper to taste

Put carrots, half the onion, and half the celery with water in a pressure cooker. Cook for 1 minute after bringing to maximum pressure. When cooled, put mixture through a blender. Sauté remaining onion and celery in ghee in a separate pan. Add carrot mixture, salt, and pepper. Stir in coconut milk and heat well, but do not boil.

67. Ishwara/Ash Gourd Soup

All gourd vegetables are extremely alkaline. The ash gourd is highly recommended, even for invalids. Gourd soups are very good for balancing the acid-alkaline state in the body.

2 cups diced ash gourd (or any
  other gourd)
1 small onion, chopped
1 stalk celery, chopped

1 tsp. grated ginger
1 tbs. ghee
2 cups water
salt and pepper to taste

Peel and dice the gourd. Put gourd pieces in a pressure cooker with water, ginger, and half of the onion. Cook for 2 minutes after reaching full pressure. Put through a blender and keep aside. In a separate pan, sauté the remaining onion and celery in ghee. Add the gourd mixture and salt and pepper to taste.

68. Uddhava/Pineapple Soup

2 cups diced fresh pineapple
  (with core and skin), or
  4 cups fresh pineapple juice

1 tsp. fresh cumin powder
a pinch of asafoetida
a pinch of fenugreek powder

1/2 tsp. honey
1 tsp. butter

4 cups water
salt and pepper to taste

Boil the diced pineapple with core and skin in 4 cups water for 5 minutes. Remove and put through a blender on low. Strain and set aside. If pineapple juice is being used, omit this step. Add pepper, salt, and spices to the juice and bring to a boil. Remove from the heat, add honey and butter, and serve.

69. Jeeva/Beetroot Soup
1 large uncooked beetroot
2 small onions, chopped
2 cups fresh yogurt
1 tbs. chopped mint leaves

1 bay leaf
water to cover
pepper and salt to taste

Wash and trim the beetroot and put it in a pressure cooker. Cover with water and cook for 2 minutes after bringing to maximum pressure. Remove and peel. Chop beetroot, add stock, and put through a blender. Return to pan and add onion, pepper, salt, and bay leaf. Simmer until onion is tender. Remove from heat and stir in 2 cups of yogurt. Sprinkle with chopped mint and serve.

70. Jnana/Chickpea Broth
1 cup chickpeas, soaked in 2 cups
   water overnight
4 cups of water.
1 onion, chopped

1 tbs. chopped scallions
1/4 tsp. cumin powder
pepper, salt, lemon juice to taste
1 tbs. ghee

Clean and drained soaked beans and discard soaking water. Put beans, 4 cups of water, and 1 onion in a pressure cooker. Cook for 15 minutes on low heat after bringing to maximum pressure. Cool, blend, and set aside. In a separate pan, sauté the scallions in ghee. Add the bean mixture and remaining ingredients. Serve hot with a few drops of lemon juice.

71. Jagadeeshwara/Soya Bean Soup (Serves 6)

1 cup soya beans, soaked overnight in 2 cups water	2 tbs. onion, chopped
1/2 cup barley	1 tsp. grated ginger
1 cup fresh mushrooms, diced	1 carrot, sliced in 2" strips
2 stalks celery, chopped	1 tbs. vegetable oil
2 tbs. chopped scallions	1 tbs. soya sauce
	5 cups water

Clean and drain soaked soya beans and discard the soaking water. Wash barley and add to soya beans. Put barley, soya beans, mushrooms, and onions with 5 cups of water in a pressure cooker and bring to maximum pressure. Reduce heat and cook for half an hour. In the meantime, in a pan large enough to hold 10 cups of liquid, sauté onions and celery in oil for a minute. Add carrot strips and sauté for 3 more minutes. Then add the soya bean/barley mixture, salt, ginger, and soya sauce. Sprinkle with chopped scallions and serve hot.

Chapter Seven: Krishna Chutneys & Pickles

Chutneys and pickles are a must in traditional Indian cuisine. They lend extra spice and accent to a variety of dishes.

72. Keshava/Tomato Chutney (12-ounce Jar)

2 cups ripe tomatoes, chopped	1 tbs. molasses or honey
1 cup fresh coriander leaves	1/4 cup water
2 tsp. grated ginger	1 tsp. salt
1 small jalapeno	

Put all ingredients through a blender. This chutney—like most other chutneys—can be used as a side dish with rice or chapatis, or as a dip.

73. Karma/Spicy Tomato Spread (Two 12-ounce Jars)

2 lbs. ripe tomatoes
2 cups sesame oil (not dark)
2 tbs. black mustard seeds
2 tbs. split urad dal, without skin
1/2 tbs. red chili powder
1/2 tsp. powdered asafoetida
1 tsp. fenugreek powder (methi)
2 tbs. molasses
1 large onion, minced
1 tbs. molasses
1 tsp. turmeric powder
1 tbs. salt

Chop tomatoes and purée in a blender without adding water. Strain and remove seed and skin. Heat oil in a heavy bottomed pan and add the mustard seeds. When they sputter, add urad dal. Add the remaining seasonings and stir for 2 minutes. Stir in the tomato purée and reduce heat. Keep stirring until all the liquid evaporates, about half an hour. When the mixture turns dark and the oil comes to the surface, it can be cooled and bottled. This spread will keep well in the refrigerator or a cool place for a month. It can be used as a sandwich spread, or as a side dish with chapatis and rice.

74. Kama/Mixed Vegetable Chutney (Serves 4)

1 large carrot, chopped
1/2 white radish, chopped
1 large ripe tomato, chopped
2 tbs. grated coconut
1 jalapeno chili
1 tsp. grated ginger
2 tbs. chopped coriander
  leaves
1/2 cup yogurt
1 tsp. salt

Put all ingredients through a blender at high speed. This chutney may be eaten with rice or chapatis.

The first thing to better health is to become vegetarian, then perhaps a stage further is to renounce even dairy produce. Then to renounce cooked things and live only on raw salads, fruit, honey, and juices.

—Dr. Barbara Moore

51

75. Kausthubha/Date Chutney (Serves 4)

1 cup dried, seedless dates	1 cup hot water
1 tsp. grated ginger	1/2 tsp. salt
1 tbs. lemon juice	

Soak dates in hot water for an hour and discard water. Put all ingredients through a blender on low to form a smooth paste. Raisins can be used instead of dates. This chutney can be used as a sandwich spread, or with rice and curry.

76. Kaumodaki/Pineapple Delight (Serves 4)

2 cups fresh pineapple, chopped	1 small jalapeno chili
1/2 cup freshly grated coconut	1/2 tsp. grated ginger
1 cup yogurt	1 cup water
1 tsp. mustard seeds	1/2 tsp. salt

With an electric grinder, grind the coconut, mustard seeds, green chili, ginger, and salt. Combine mixture with the yogurt. In the meantime, cook the pineapple in water, covered, over low heat for 5 minutes. Mash lightly with a wooden spoon and add to the yogurt sauce. Mix well, heat, and take off the stove before mixture comes to a boil.

77. Kanayya/Sweet Mango Chutney (Serves 4)

1 large, raw green mango	1/4 cup water
1/2 tsp. chili powder	1/2 tsp. salt
2 tbs. jaggery	

Remove pit and skin from the mango. Chop flesh into pieces. Blend all ingredients into a fine paste with a blender. This chutney can be served with either rice and curry, or chapatis and curry.

78. Mukunda/Apple Chutney (Serves 4)

2 slightly sour, raw green apples
2 tbs. jaggery
pinch of red chili powder
pinch of salt

Remove seeds from the apples and chop. Put apples and the remaining ingredients through a blender until a smooth paste is formed.

79. Muraree/Sour Mango Chutney (Serves 4)

1 large, raw green mango
1 jalapeno chili
2 tbs. grated coconut
1 tsp. chopped onion
3 tbs. water
1/2 tsp. salt

Remove the pit and skin from the mango and chop flesh into bits. Put mango and all other ingredients through a blender until a fine paste is formed.

80. Madhava/Mango Chutney (Serves 4)

1 cup green mangoes, chopped
1/2 cup fresh mint leaves
1/4 cup grated coconut
1 tsp. black mustard seeds
3 tbs. yogurt
1 tbs. chopped onion
1 tsp. grated ginger
1 small jalapeno chili
1/2 tsp. salt

Put all ingredients through a blender and serve as a side dish. Since all chutneys are uncooked they provide extra nutrition, as well as a bit of spice, to ordinary fare.

81. Moksha/Mango Pickle (Two 10-ounce Jars)

5 large, raw green mangoes
2 tsp. red chili powder
4 tbs. salt
1 tsp. black mustard seeds

Better to hunt in fields
for health unbought,
Than fee the doctor for
a nauseous draught.
The wise for cure on
exercise depend.
God never made his
work for man to mend.

—JOHN DRYDEN

1/2 tsp. asafoetida powder   1 tsp. turmeric powder
1 tsp. fenugreek powder   1 tbs. natural vinegar
1/2 cup sesame oil (not dark)

Remove pit and skin from mangoes and cut flesh into small pieces. Stir salt into mixture and put in the sun for a day, stirring occasionally. Leave overnight in a covered stoneware jar. Next day heat the oil in a heavy bottomed wok; add mustard seeds and cook until they sputter. Mix in the three powders and stir for 2 minutes. Add the mango pieces along with the liquid that accumulated in the jar. Cook for a minute and remove from heat. Cool and add vinegar. This pickle can be bottled and kept for a month.

Lime pickle can be made in exactly the same way using limes instead of mangoes. The limes should be quartered and salted and kept in the sun for a day, as with the mangoes. While the mango pickle can be used immediately, the lime pickle has to be kept for at least two weeks before using, or until the skins become soft.

82. Mantra/Coconut Chutney (Serves 4)
1 cup fresh grated coconut   1 tsp. jaggery or honey
1 cup mint or coriander leaves   1/2 cup water
1 small jalapeno chili   1/2 tsp. salt
1/2 tsp. lemon juice

Put all ingredients through a blender at high speed until smooth. This chutney is generally used in South India with a special dish called *iddlies* and with rice pancakes called dosas. It would also go well with either rice or chapatis.

While bread has often been called the staff of life in the West, the bread we get on the market these days often proves to be just the opposite. The staff becomes a stick to beat the life out of us! Actually one can exist just as well without bread; chapatis are a good substitute. But if bread has to be eaten at all, it is best baked at home using good whole wheat flour, preferably pounded by hand. The following recipe yields excellent results. Nut loaves are also nourishing and make a pleasant change from the usual fare. Stainless steel pans are recommended. (See page 10 for more about flours.)

83. Mitra (Whole Wheat) Bread (2 Medium-sized Loaves)
Part 1

4 cups whole wheat flour
2 cups lukewarm water
1/2 cup fresh milk, slightly heated

1/2 cup jaggery
1 heaping tbs. active dry yeast
2 medium-sized pans, oiled

Pour the lukewarm water into a large stoneware bowl. Add the jaggery and stir. Sprinkle yeast on top and stir lightly until yeast is completely dissolved. Add the warm milk and stir well. Now fold in one cup of flour at a time with a wooden spoon; use an upward rotary motion, to incorporate the air and to make the mixture smooth and elastic. Use about 100 strokes. Cover the bowl with a damp cloth and place in the sun or in a warm place (85° to 100°F.). Allow to rise for 45 minutes.

Part 2

4 tbs. butter, melted and cooled
1 tbs. salt

3 cups whole wheat flour

When batter has risen to almost double in size, add the melted butter and salt; fold in by stirring around the sides of the bowl. Then fold in half a cup of flour at a time, until dough no longer sticks to bottom of the bowl. This should be done gently without tearing the dough. Turn the ball of dough out onto a floured board or marble-topped table. Keep hands and board well-floured; gradually incorporate all the flour until the dough no longer sticks to the board or hands when kneading. Use more flour if necessary, but add a little at a time.

Knead well for 10 minutes until dough forms a smooth ball. Oil the bowl, place the ball of dough in it; press down to fit dough into bowl. Now take dough out, turn it over, and re-place it in the bowl. Press again to fit the bowl. Cover dough with a damp cloth and put it back in the sun or a warm place to rise again for another half an hour or 45 minutes, or until it doubles in size.

Part 3

Punch the dough down several times with your fist. Turn it out on to a board and knead a few times more. Divide dough into two equal halves. Flatten one half a little with your hands and then roll it up like a carpet. Press the side and middle seams together. Place the dough inside one of the oiled pans, seam-side up. Flatten dough down to fit the pan. Turn it out of the pan and return it, seam-side down. Flatten again to fit pan. Repeat procedure with the remaining dough. Cover pans with a damp cloth and return to a warm place. Allow breads to rise for another half hour, or until dough fills the pan. Even if it rises a little above the pan, it does not matter. Lightly puncture the middle of each loaf with a knife. Brush each top lightly with oil and sprinkle with sesame seeds. Bake at 350°F. for half an hour to 45 minutes. If the bread sounds hollow when top is thumped upon, it is done. Remove from pan when ready and cool on a wire tray. Slice only after cooling.

84. Murali/Vegetable Loaf (Serves 4)

2 cups grated carrots
2 cups cooked potatoes, lightly mashed
1 cup chopped green beans, steamed
3 tbs. whole wheat flour
1 onion, minced
2 cups coconut milk (or vegetable stock)
1/2 tsp. black pepper powder
5 tbs. butter
1 cup paneer, cubed (see p. 20)
1 tsp. garam masala (see p. 23)
1 tsp. salt

Melt butter in a pan and sauté the onion. Mix in flour and milk. Add seasoning and cook until thick, stirring constantly to prevent lumping. Slowly add paneer cubes. Put cooked vegetables into an oiled baking dish and cover with the sauce. Bake at 350°F. for half an hour.

85. Madhusudhan/Vegetable Bread (Serves 4)

1 cup whole wheat flour, or corn flour
1/2 tsp. baking powder
3 cups finely grated or chopped vegetables
  (carrots, green beans, cauliflower, etc.)
2 cups thin nut milk (cashew, almond,
  or coconut)
1 small onion, minced
1 tbs. savory herbs (majoram, sage, and chives or cumin, cloves, and cinnamon)
1 tbs. chopped parsley (or coriander)
2 tsp. salt

Sieve flour and baking powder together first, then fold into the nut milk. Add herbs and salt and mix well. Toss in vegetables and mix well. Put into an oiled baking dish and bake at 400°F. for half an hour.

86. Madana/Peanut Loaf (Serves 4)

2 cups roasted peanuts
2 cups pounded rice, wheat, or oats
2 cups fresh tomato juice
1 onion, minced
3 tbs. whole wheat flour
1/2 tsp. salt
1/2 cup water

To make tomato juice, put tomatoes and water through a blender and strain. To make the loaf, coarsely grind peanuts. Add salt to the juice and mix in flour, pounded grain, and onion. Bake in oiled dish for half an hour at 300°F.

87. Manohar/Sweet Nut Loaf (Serves 4)

1 cup almonds
1/2 cup pounded whole wheat
  or pounded rice

2 ripe bananas
1 cup seedless raisins
1/2 cup coconut milk (or water)

Grind almonds in an electric grinder and mash the bananas. Mix all the ingredients together and put in a greased bread pan. Bake at 400° F. for a half an hour.

88. Madhuvan/Rice Nut Loaf (Serves 4)

1 cup almonds
2 cups boiled rice
1 cup nut milk

1 tsp. black pepper
1/2 tsp. garam masala
1 tsp. salt

Coarsly grind the almonds with a mortar and pestle or electric grinder. Mix all the ingredients together and put into an oiled bread pan. Bake at 400°F. for half an hour.

89. Maharishi/Savory Loaf (Serves 2)

1 cup roasted peanuts, finely ground
1 bunch spinach
1 onion, chopped
2 tbs. coriander or parsley

1 cup pounded wheat or rice
1/2 cup water
1/2 tsp. black pepper
1 tsp. salt

Boil spinach lightly in water and mash. Add the remaining ingredients and mix well. Put into a greased pan. Bake at 400°F. for half an hour.

Food is the universal medicine, because creatures came into existence out of food, which preceded them in the order of creation.

—TAITTIRIYA UPANISHAD

Chapatis, a type of unleavened bread made with whole wheat flour, are commonly eaten all over North India. Chapatis are much more nourishing than bread made with white flour. The only utensil needed for making them is a chapati *tawa,* which is a shallow heavy-bottomed iron plate, something like a hot plate but slightly curved at the bottom. If this is not available, chapatis could be made in a heavy, flat-bottomed pan or griddle.

90. Muni/Plain Chapatis
2 cups chapati flour (see p. 10)
3/4 cup luke warm water

This recipe will make about 6 to 8 chapatis. As a general rule, use 1 heaping tablespoon of flour for each chapati.

Place flour in a bowl and make a hole in the center. Pour a little water in the hole and fold in flour from the sides with your hands. Keep adding water and tossing lightly until the flour forms a ball and does not stick to either your hands or the bowl. Turn dough out on a floured board and knead well until smooth. Place ball of dough in an oiled bowl and cover with a damp cloth for 1 to 2 hours. Shape dough into 4 to 6 balls; flatten balls with your hands into round patties. Use as much flour as needed to keep the balls from sticking. Roll patties out on a floured board so they are fairly thin. In the meantime, heat the chapati *tawa* or heavy bottomed pan. Place a chapati on the hot *tawa* and flip over after 1 minute. Flip over again after 2 minutes. Keep a soft cloth ball ready and press the chapati lightly with the cloth as it starts to rise. Press gently and firmly so that the whole chapati rises up like a skin.

Heat should be carefully regulated so that the chapati does not burn or become too crisp: it should be soft and light in color. Repeat until all chapatis are cooked. Line a serving dish with a large cloth napkin to place them in as they are made, and cover with the ends of the napkin. This will ensure that the chapatis remain soft and pliable until the whole batch is finished and ready to serve.

Note: Chapatis can be made even more nourishing by adding some greens to the dough. Chop the greens—like spinach, coriander, parsley, mint, scallions—fine and insert a small amount into balls before they are rolled out. These balls will be slightly thicker than ordinary chapatis balls.

Paratha is a griddle-fried whole wheat bread.
91. Maya/Potato Parathas (Makes 6 to 10)

4 cups chapati flour
4 medium-sized potatoes
1 onion, minced
2 tbs. fresh coriander leaves,
   chopped

2 tsp. cumin powder
1/2 tsp. black pepper powder
1 tsp. salt
2 cups water

Prepare dough according to chapati recipe. In the meantime, boil potatoes in their jackets. When cooled, remove the skin and mash well. Add the remaining ingredients to the potato mash. Mix well and make 10 balls with the potato mix, about half the size of the dough balls.

   Make 10 balls with chapati dough. Flatten ball slightly between your palms, making a depression in the center. Place potato ball in the depression and fold dough over so that it covers the potato ball. Press ball in your hand to make a circular patty; place patty on floured board and roll out to a 1/4" thickness. Follow same procedure for remaining 9 balls. With a bit of practice the filling can be placed evenly so that the potato mix will not come out of the dough when it is rolled. Heat the

60

chapati *tawa* or skillet and cook *paratha* on both sides, until it turns a light brown. Brush with a little ghee before turning it over. Serve with any of the chutney or curry recipes given in this book.

92. Nishkama/Radish Parathas (Makes 10)

4 cups chapati flour	1-1/2 cups water
2 large white radishes *(mooli),* finely grated	2 tbs. minced onion
	1 tsp. salt
1 tsp. cumin powder	1/2 tsp. black pepper powder

Prepare dough according to the chapati recipe.

Squeeze out as much liquid from the grated radishes as possible. Add remaining ingredients to the radishes, mix well, and divide into 10 parts. Make ten balls with the chapati dough and follow instructions in preceding recipe. Be sure that the filling is completely dry; if any liquid accumulates, the *parathas* will be spoiled. Serve with any salad that has a yogurt dressing, as well as with any chutney or curry.

93. Nirmala/Lentil Parathas *(*Makes 10)

4 cups whole wheat flour	1-1/2 cups water
1/2 cup lentils or moong dal	1 tbs. minced onion
1 tsp. cumin powder	1 tbs. chopped coriander leaves
1/2 tsp. black pepper powder	1 tsp. salt

Prepare dough according to the chapati recipe, shape into 10 balls, and set aside.

Put lentils in a pressure cooker and cook for 3 minutes after bringing to maximum pressure. Uncover and cook until the liquid evaporates. Add remaining ingredients and mix well. The mixture should be quite dry. Make 10 balls out of the lentil mixture and proceed to combine them with the chapati balls, according to the Potato *Paratha* recipe.

94. Naivedya/Cheese Parathas (Makes 10)

4 cups chapati flour	1 tbs. minced onion
1 cup soft cheese (see p. 19)	1/4 tsp. turmeric powder
1 tomato	1 tbs. ghee
2 tsp. aniseed	

Prepare dough according to the chapati recipe, shape into 10 balls, and set aside.

Heat ghee in a pan and sauté onions for 2 minutes. Add the remaining ingredients and sauté until the water evaporates. Set cheese mixture aside to cool. Then flatten chapati balls into patties, each about 5" in diameter. Place one tenth of cheese mixture on one half of patty, making sure it is not too close to the edge. Fold the patty in half. Press the edges together, making sure there are no air bubbles inside. Fold the semi-circle in half again, so as to form something resembling a triangle. Press the edges together and brush both sides with ghee. Repeat for remaining 9 balls and cook in hot *tawa,* onto which a little ghee has been smeared, until *parathas* are golden brown on each side.

Chapter Ten: Narayana Rice Dishes

Rice is a versatile grain and can produce a wide variety of dishes quickly, especially if one has a pressure cooker or rice cooker. Rice is India's most important grain; it is the staple diet in the South and is widely used in the North. The highly polished long-grained variety found in the North, though good to look at, is not nearly as nutritive as the unpolished, perfectly hand-pounded variety from the South, which is slightly red in color. In Vanamali cooking, we always try to use the unpolished variety. Plain rice is generally served with a curry, a salad, and perhaps a woked vegetable. On special occasions more than one curry can be served and perhaps some *pappadam* (dal waffers), as well as a sweet for dessert. Many exotic food combinations are possible using rice as a base. Basmati and brown rice are both delicious and nutritive.

Since the qualities differ with each rice, it is difficult to give exact cooking times for rice. It also depends on one's personal taste—some people prefer rice soft, others prefer it a bit harder. Rice that has matured for over a year will need more water and more cooking time. Long-grained rice, like Basmati, needs less water and time. The timing given in the recipes that follow are for Basmati rice. If you are using another type, please adjust the time accordingly.

Plain Rice with a Pressure Cooker (Serves 4)

1 cup rice, cleaned   1/2 tsp. salt
1-3/4 cups water

Boil water in body of the pressure cooker. Add cleaned rice and salt. Cover and bring cooker to maximum pressure. Reduce heat and cook for 1 minute. Remove from heat and allow to cool for 10 minutes before removing lid.

Plain Rice without a Pressure Cooker (Serves 4)

1 cup rice, cleaned   1/2 tsp. salt
2 cups water

Boil the water and add rice. Cover halfway with the lid to prevent boiling over. Reduce heat until water evaporates. Taste to see if rice is cooked. After cooking, turn off heat and leave covered for 10 minutes to absorb any leftover moisture.

The foods that are bitter, sour, saltish, hot pungent, dry, and burning, which produce pain, grief and disease are dear to the rajasic nature.

—BHAGAVAD GITA,
CHAPTER 17, VERSE 9

95. Paramatma/Vegetable Pulau (Serves 4 to 6)

2 cups rice, washed and drained
2 pieces cinnamon, 1" each
2 cups mixed vegetables, chopped
   (carrots, cauliflower, peas, French
   green beans, etc.)
4 black cardamon pods
6 cloves
3 tsp. salt
2 bay leaves
1 tsp. chopped cashews
1 tbs. raisins
1 onion, chopped
1 tsp. turmeric powder
2 tbs. ghee
3-1/2 cups water

This pulau can be made either with all these vegetables or with a combination of one or more of them depending on availability.

Heat ghee in a pressure cooker and sauté cashews and raisins; remove from pan and set aside. Sauté onions, then remove from pan and set aside. In the remaining ghee, add cinnamon, cardamom pods, cloves, bay leaves, and cumin and sauté for 2 minutes. Add turmeric and chopped vegetables and cook another 3 minutes. Add the rice and cook for another minute. Mix in water and salt. Place lid on pressure cooker and cook for 1 minute after bringing to maximum pressure. Allow to cool gradually before opening. Place pulau in a serving dish and sprinkle with cashews, raisins, and onion.

96. Pundareekaksha/Cheese Pulau (Serves 4 to 6)

2 cups rice, washed and drained
1 cup paneer cubes
2 black cardamom pods
2 pieces cinnamon, 1" each
5 cloves
2 bay leaves
5 peppercorns
2 tbs. ghee
3-1/2 cups water
2 tsp. salt
1 tsp. turmeric powder
1 onion, chopped

Sauté the onion in ghee until translucent, then brown paneer pieces, remove from pan and set aside. Follow instructions for vegetable pulau given in preceding recipe. After removing pulau from the pressure cooker, garnish with paneer cubes instead of raisins and nuts.

97. Pushpanjali/Peas Pulau (Serves 4 to 6)
Substitute one cup of fresh garden peas or 1 cup sprouted chick peas for the paneer; all other ingredients are exactly the same as for the preceding recipe. Add the peas or chickpeas to the rice before cooking.

98. Parthasarathi/Tomato Rice (Serves 4 to 6)

2 cups rice, washed and drained	2 pieces cinnamon, 1" each
1 cup tomato juice	5 cloves
2-1/2 cups coconut milk	1 jalapeno chili, chopped
1/4 cup ghee	1 onion, sliced into rings
3 cardamom pods	2 tsp. salt
black 1 tsp. turmeric powder	2 tbs. chopped coriander

Heat ghee in a pressure cooker and fry onion slices, cardamom pods, cinnamon, and cloves. Add coconut milk, tomato juice, chili, salt, and turmeric. Add the rice, cover, and cook for 1 minutes after bringing to maximum pressure. Remove from heat and allow to cool for 10 minutes before removing lid. Sprinke with chopped coriander and serve.

99. Padmanabha/Green Pulau (Serves 4 to 6)

2 cups rice, washed and drained	2 tbs. ghee or butter
3-1/2 cups water	1 onion, chopped
1 bunch fresh coriander, chopped	1 tsp. turmeric powder
1 bunch fresh spinach, chopped	1 tomato, sliced
2 tbs. garam masala (see p. 23)	

Heat ghee in a pressure cooker and sauté onion. Add garam masala and turmeric and cook for a minute. Mix in rice and cook for another minute. Add water and cover. Bring to maximum pressure and cook for 1 minute. Remove pressure cooker from heat and allow to cool for 10 minutes before uncovering. In the meantime, chop spinach and lightly steam. When rice is cooled, add the steamed spinach and coriander leaves, and toss well. Spinach should not be overcooked or contain any liquid. Serve with sprigs of coriander and tomato slices.

100. Pavithra/South Indian Masala Rice (Serves 4 to 6)

2 cups rice	1 tsp. coriander powder
1/2 cup chopped carrots	1/2 tsp. fenugreek powder
1/2 cup chopped green beans	1 tsp. turmeric powder
1 cup lentils	1 cup tomato juice
1/4 cup chopped pumpkin	1 tbs. lemon juice
1/2 cup fresh peas	2 tbs. ghee
1 onion, chopped	5 cups water
1 tsp. chopped jalapeno chili	2 tsp. salt
1 tsp. garam masala (see p. 23)	coriander leaves, for garnish

Clean and wash rice and lentils; drain them very well, so that no water remains. Heat 1 tablespoon of ghee in pressure cooker and sauté the onion and green chili. Add coriander and fenugreek powders and stir well. Add the rice and lentils and stir fry for 2 minutes. Stir in 4 cups water, salt, and turmeric powder. Cover and cook for 2 minutes after bringing to maximum pressure. Remove from heat and allow to cool for 10 minutes before removing lid.

In the meantime, cook the vegetables in 1 cup of water in a separate pan, covered. Keep the cooking water from the vegetables aside to use later in soups. In another large pan, heat remaining tablespoon of ghee and stir in the garam masala. Then add the rice-lentil mixture, vegetables, tomato juice, and lemon juice. Mix well and cover with a tight-fitting lid. Place on low heat for about 3 minutes. Remove from the heat, sprinkle with coriander leaves and serve.

101. Purusha/Nut Rice (Serves 4 to 6)

2 cups cooked rice
1 tbs. chopped cashews
1 tbs. raisins
1 onion, sliced
1 piece of cinnamon, 1"
1/4 cup ghee
1 tsp. salt

In a large pan, heat ghee. Fry onion, remove, and set aside. Fry cinnamon, cashews and raisins. Reduce heat and add cooked rice, onion, and salt. Mix well and serve.

102. Prakriti/Sweet Corn Rice (Serves 4 to 6)

2 cups cooked rice
1 cup cooked sweet corn
1 tbs. chopped cashews
2 tbs. ghee
1 piece of cinnamon, 1"
1 tsp. salt

In large pan, heat ghee and fry the cashews and cinnamon. Add the remaining ingredients, mix well, and serve.

103. Rishi/Mango Rice (Serves 4 to 6)

2 cups cooked rice
1 cup grated coconut
1/2 cup grated green mango
1 tsp. black mustard seeds
1/4 tsp. asafoetida powder
1 tsp. turmeric powder
1/2 jalapeno chili, chopped
2 tsp. salt
1 tsp. each split moong dal
  and black dal
2 tbs. ghee

Soak the dals in water for half an hour; drain and dry. Grind the mango, mustard, asafoetida, turmeric, and chili in an electric grinder. Heat ghee in a large pan and sauté dried dals. Add rice, salt, and ground mango mixture. Mix well. Add grated coconut and toss well. Serve with mango chutney.

104. Parikshit/Lemon Rice (Serves 4 to 6)

2 cups cooked rice	1/2 tsp. black mustard seeds
4 tbs. lemon juice	1/2 tsp. sesame seeds
1 tsp. turmeric powder	2 tbs. ghee
1/4 tsp. fenugreek powder	2 tsp. salt
1/4 tsp. asafoetida powder	

In a large pan, heat the ghee and cook the mustard seeds until they sputter. Turn off the heat, add remaining ingredients—rice last—and toss well. Serve hot, decorated with lemon rings, lime pickle, and salad.

105. Arati/Fruit Pulau (Serves 4 to 6)

2 cups rice	a pinch of mace
3-1/2 cups coconut milk	1 tsp. chopped nutmeg
1 cup cherries, pineapple chunks, or seedless grapes	1/2 tsp. salt
1 onion, sliced	2 tbs. ghee
	sweet chutney

Cook rice in coconut milk and set aside. Heat ghee in a pan and sauté onion. Remove from heat and blend in mace and nutmeg. Then add rice and fruits and mix well. Serve with sweet chutney and arrange fresh cherries or pineapple rings around edges of the dish.

106. Pradyumna/Coconut Rice (Serves 4 to 6)

2 cups rice
3-1/2 cups coconut milk
1 onion, sliced

1 cup nuts (peanuts, pistachios,
  cashews, or almonds)
2 tbs. ghee

Cook rice in coconut milk and set aside. Heat ghee in a large pan and sauté the onion. Add nuts and cook for 2 more minutes. Stir in rice and mix well. Serve garnished with nuts.

107. Anirudha/Italian Risotto (Serves 4 to 6)

2 cups cooked rice
1 cup broccoli flowerettes
1 carrot, diced
2 green bell peppers, sliced
1/2 cup mushrooms
2 tomatoes, chopped
1/4 cup olive oil
1 onion, chopped

1/2 cup shredded Parmesan cheese
1/4 cup wholewheat bread
  crumbs
2 tsp. salt
2 tsp. aniseed
1 tsp. oregano
1/4 tsp. black pepper powder

Partially steam broccoli and carrots. Heat oil in pan and add aniseed and oregano. Mix in tomatoes and sauté. Add vegetables and all remaining ingredients, except the cheese. Transfer to a casserole dish and cover with cheese and breadcrumbs. Top with oil or a dollop of butter, cover, and bake at 300°F. for 10 minutes. Uncover for last 2 minutes and serve immediately.

108. Divya/Chinese Fried Rice (Serves 4 to 6)

2 cups cooked rice
5 tbs. sesame oil (not dark)

1/2 cup cubed tofu or soya
  milk cheese

2 green bell peppers, thinly sliced
1/2 cup black mushrooms
1 cup moong beans, sprouted
1 carrot, cut into strips
1 cup thinly sliced cabbage
2 chopped scallions

1 large onion, sliced and quartered
2 celery stalks, sliced
1/4 cup sliced almonds
1/4 tsp. freshly grated ginger
4 tbs. soya sauce
1/2 tsp. salt

Heat oil in a large pan. Add the onions and ginger and fry for 1 minute. Add the vegetables and stir fry for 5 minuutes. Mix in the bean sprouts and fry another minute, then do the same with the almonds. Add soya sauce and stir well. Turn off heat and add the cooked rice. Toss well; decorate with tofu and serve with soya sauce.

109. Aryan/Spanish Rice (Serves 4 to 6)

2 cups rice, slightly undercooked
2 tbs. chopped onion
1 cup chopped green bell pepper
1 tbs. oil

1 tsp. red chili powder (optional)
1/4 cup homemade tomato sauce
1 tbs. sesame seeds

Heat oil in a large pan and sauté onion for 1 minute. Add sesame seeds and fry. Mix in chopped bell pepper and cook for another minute. Add tomato sauce and chili powder and simmer a few minutes. Put rice in and keep stirring until the rice is evenly coated. Remove from the heat and serve immediately. For a less spicy dish, do not add the red chili powder.

110. Bhagavan/Pineapple Rice (Serves 4 to 6)

2 cups rice
1-1/2 cup water
2 cups pineapple juice
1 cup freshly chopped pineapple cubes

4 sprigs parsley or coriander
2 lemon slices
1/2 tsp. cardamom powder

Put rice, pineapple juice, and water in a pressure cooker. Reduce heat and cook for 1 minute after bringing to maximum pressure. Remove from heat and allow to cool 10 minutes before removing lid. In a large bowl, combine rice, pineapple chunks, cardamom powder, and greens. Decorate with lemon slices and serve with pineapple or date chutney.

111. Nirguna/Indonesian Rice (Serves 4 to 6)

2 cups rice, washed	1 onion, sliced
2-1/2 cups coconut milk	1 tsp. turmeric powder
1 cup water	1 tsp. salt
1 bay leaf	1 cucumber, sliced
2 tbs. chopped celery	1 red bell pepper

In a pressure cooker, bring the coconut milk, water, turmeric, and bay leaf to a boil. Add rice and salt, cover, and reduce heat. Cook for 2 minutes after bringing to maximum pressure. Allow to cool for 10 minutes before removing lid. Turn mixture into a serving dish and garnish with celery, sliced cucumber, and onion. Cut red pepper into the shape of a flower and place in the center of dish as a garnish.

112. Yogeshwara/Spanish Rice (Serves 4 to 6)

2 cups rice, washed	1 onion, chopped
2 cups sliced tomatoes	1 cup vegetable stock
1/2 cup tomato puree	1 tbs. oil
2 cups water	1/2 tsp. salt
1 red chili pepper, sliced	

Cook rice in pressure cooker with water and vegetable stock for 1 minute after bringing to full pressure. Fry the onion and pepper in oil. Remove rice from heat and allow to cool for 10 minutes before

The body does not require any medicine provided one eats only after the previous meal has been fully digested and assimilated.

—Saint Thiruvalluvar

71

removing lid. In a bowl combine rice with tomato puree, fried onions and pepper, and salt. Layer the rice mixture and tomato slices in a baking dish and bake for 10 minutes at 400°F.

113. Homa/Balkan Rice (Serves 4 to 6)

2 cups cooked rice	1 lb. tomatoes, sliced
2 jalapeno chilies	1 tsp. black pepper powder
4 onions, sliced	1/4 cup oil
1 cup chopped nuts (cashews, peanuts, or almonds)	1 tsp. salt

Heat oil in a large pan and sauté the onions. Add salt, pepper, jalapeno chilies, and rice. Place half of the rice mixture in a casserole dish, then add a layer of nuts and a layer of tomatoes. Top with the remaining rice and then the remaining tomatoes. Cover and cook at 250°F. for half an hour. The finished product will resemble a rice sandwich with a nut filling.

Chapter Eleven: Nanda Kumar Curries

A curry is a preparation of vegetables or meat containing a gravy-like sauce. Different parts of India have different varieties of curries. Most curries contain a lot of hot chili powder and spices, which make them too hot for Western palates. At Vanamali we try to adapt the traditional curries to suit the Nature Care Program. True nature care demands that food be eaten as raw and natural as possible, without additives, such as spices. But our palate demands tasty food. The Indian palate especially is used to hot, spicy, pungent foods. In these recipes we have tried to strike a happy, and tasty, medium between spicy and natural. Those who are used to hot curries may find our variations a bit bland, but those whose taste buds have not been spoiled by over indulgence in rajasic food will find that these recipes provide variety while being nutritious and appetizing at the same time.

The following recipes will serve 4 to 6 people.

114. Shyam/Sambar

Sambar *is a traditional and well-known South Indian curry. Eggplant and okra are the two vegetables most commonly used to make* sam-bar, *but being a versatile dish it will taste equally good with carrots, radishes, turnips, or even plain shallots.*

1 cup toovar dal, washed	1/2 tsp. turmeric powder
1/2 cup chopped eggplant	3 tbs. lemon juice
1/2 cup okra pods, cut in 1" pieces	6 cups water
2 ripe tomatoes, chopped	7 tbs. oil
2 tbs. coriander or curry leaves	1 tbs. jaggery
1/2 tsp. black mustard seed	

Cook dal in pressure cooker with 4 cups of water for 5 minutes after bringing to maximum pressure. In a separate pan, sauté the okra pods and eggplant pieces in 1 tablespoon of oil for 3 minutes. Add 2 cups of water, salt, and turmeric and boil until vegetables are almost cooked. Mix the ground masala (below) with the cooked dal and add to the vegetables. Add the tomatoes and simmer for another few minutes. Heat remaining oil in a frying pan and cook mustard seeds until they splutter. Pour them into the curry and add jaggery and lemon juice. Garnish with coriander leaves or curry leaves.

Sambar Masala

2 dried, whole red chilis (hot)	1/2 tsp. fenugreek seeds
3 tbs. freshly grated coconut	1/4 tsp. asafoetida
2 tbs. coriander seeds	1 tsp. salt

Lightly fry the above ingredients without oil, grind in an electric grinder, and add to the cooked dal.

115. Sannyas/Aviyal or Mixed Vegetable Curry

Aviyal is a curry made with a mixture of different South Indian vegetables. We have listed a variety of vegetables from which five or six may be used, depending on availability.

1/2 cup raw, green plantains	1/2 cup potatoes
1/2 cup snake gourd	1-1/2 cups soured yogurt
1/2 cup pumpkin	1 tsp. salt
1/2 cup ash gourd	1 tsp. turmeric powder
1/2 cup green papaya	1 tbs. curry leaves
1/2 cup carrots	2 tbs. unsalted butter
1/2 cup green beans	2 cups of water
1/2 cup turnips	

Remove skin from all the vegetables and chop into 2" pieces, each 1/2" thick. Mix the masala (below) into the yogurt, stir well, and set aside.

In a large flat-bottomed pan, cook the vegetables and fruits with salt and turmeric in water on high heat. When vegetables are almost cooked, add the masala and mix well. When just about to boil, remove mixture from the heat. Season with butter and garnish with curry leaves. This curry should be fairly thick.

Masala

1/2 cup freshly grated coconut	
1 tbs. chopped onion	1 jalapeno chili
	1/2 tsp. cumin seeds

Grind all ingredients together in an electric grinder and add to the yogurt.

116. Tyagi /Olan or Bean-Pumpkin Curry

1/2 cup red pinto beans, dried
2 cups tender pumpkin slices,
   1" x 1-1/2"
1/2 cup thick coconut milk
1 cup thin coconut milk

2 jalapeno chilies, chopped
2 cups water
1 tsp. salt
1 tbs. curry leaves
2 tbs. unsalted butter

Soak the dried beans in water overnight. The next morning, rinse the beans and place in a pressure cooker with 2 cups of water. Cover and bring to full pressure. Reduce heat and cook for 15 minutes. Remove from heat and allow to cool for 10 minutes before uncovering.

If pumpkin is green, do not remove the skin; remove seeds and pulp and keep for soup stock. If pumpkin is hard and yellow, skin should be removed before chopping.

Add pumpkin pieces, jalapeno chilies, salt, and thin coconut milk to the beans, but do not close lid tightly. Boil until the pumpkin is cooked. Add the thick coconut milk and remove from the heat before mixture boils. Season with butter and curry leaves.

117. Kalyan Yogurt Curry

1/2 cup yams or other tuber, 1/2" cubes
1/2 cup raw, green plantains, 1/2" cubes
3 cups soured yogurt
1 tsp. turmeric powder
1/2 tsp. black mustard seeds

1 tsp. salt
1 tbs. oil
1 tbs. jaggery
1 cup water

Masala

1 cup freshly grated coconut
1 tbs. black pepper pods

1 tsp. cumin seeds

Grind masala ingredients in an electric grinder and mix with yogurt. Cook vegetables in water with salt and turmeric. Add masala and remove from heat just before mixture starts to boil. Add jaggery. Heat oil in a frying pan and cook mustard seeds until they splutter; add to the curry.

118. Mangala/Vegetable-Chickpea Curry

1 cup chickpeas, soaked overnight	3 cups water
1/2 cup yams, 1/2" cubes	1 tsp. salt
1/2 cup pumpkin, 1/2" cubes	1 tsp. black pepper powder
1/4 cup raw, green plantains, cubed	1 tsp. turmeric powder
1 onion, chopped	1 tsp. split, skinned black
1/2 cup grated coconut	gram dal
2 tsp. coriander powder	1/2 tsp. black mustard seeds
2 tbs. oil	

Rinse chickpeas and place in pressure cooker with 3 cups of water. Cover and bring to full pressure. Reduce heat and cook for 15 minutes. Remove pan from heat and allow to cool before removing the lid. Uncover, add vegetables, salt, black pepper, turmeric and coriander powders. Return to high heat and cook without pressure until vegetables are done.

Heat oil in a frying pan and cook mustard seeds and black gram dal until mustard seeds sputter. Add onions and sauté for 2 minutes. Add grated coconut and sauté until the coconut turns brown and begins to emit the fragrance of fried coconut. Pour this mixture into the pressure cooker. Return to heat but do not cover. Simmer for 2 minutes. Remove from the heat and serve.

76

119. Sadharmya/Sweet Mango-Gourd Curry

4 small ripe mangoes (or 2 large)
2 cups ash gourd, bottle gourd, or other squash (not pumpkin), cubed
1 cup soured yogurt
1/2 tsp. turmeric powder

2 cups water
2 tsp. oil
1/4 tsp. fenugreek seeds
1 tsp. salt
1 tsp. jaggery

Masala
1/2 cup grated coconut
2 jalapeno chilies

1/2 tsp. black mustard seeds

Grind the masala ingredients in an electric grinder and set aside. Wash, peel, and cut mangoes into quarters. Cook the squash in 2 cups of water. When cooked, add the mango, salt, and turmeric powder. Mix ground masala with the yogurt. When vegetables are cooked, stir in the masala and bring to a boil. Remove from the heat. Heat oil in a small frying pan and cook mustard and fenugreek seeds until mustard seeds splutter. Pour into the curry and add jaggery and curry leaves.

Pachadi is a vegetable curry made with coconut, yogurt, and mustard seeds.

120. Salokya/Pumpkin Pachadi

2 cups ripe pumpkin, cubed
1 cup soured yogurt
2 cups water
1 tbs. oil

1 tsp. salt
1/2 tsp. black mustard seeds
1 tbs. curry leaves

Masala
1/2 cup grated coconut
1 tsp. black mustard seeds

1 jalapeno chili

Grind masala ingredients in an electric grinder and set aside.

Cook pumpkin in 2 cups of water. Mix ground masala with the yogurt and add mixture to the cooked pumpkin. Bring to a boil. Mix well and remove from the heat.

In a frying pan, heat oil and cook curry leaves and mustard seeds until they sputter. Season curry with this mixture.

121. Samata/Okra Pachadi

3 cups okra pods, washed, dried, and chopped in 1/2" pieces	2 tbs. oil
1 onion, chopped	1 tsp. salt
1-1/2 cup soured yogurt	1 tbs. curry leaves

Masala

1/2 cup grated coconut	1 jalapeno chili
1-1/2 tsp. black mustard seeds	

Grind masala ingredients in an electric grinder and set aside.

Heat 1-1/2 tbs. of oil in pan and sauté the okra pods and onion until golden brown, stirring continuously. Mix ground masala with the yogurt and combine with the okra pods. Add salt and cook over low heat for 5 minutes. In a frying pan, heat the remaining 1/2 tablespoon oil and cook remaining mustard seeds until they sputter. Add curry leaves and combine mixture with *pachadi*.

122. Sattva/Sweet-Sour Okra

3 cups okra, washed, dried, and chopped in 1/2" pieces	1 cup water
1 onion, chopped	1 tsp. turmeric powder
2 cups chopped tomatoes	1/4 tsp. fenugreek powder
	a pinch of asafoetida

78

1 jalapeno chili, slit
2 tbs. oil
1 tsp. jaggery

1/2 tsp. black mustard seeds
1 tsp. salt
1 tbs. chopped coriander leaves

Blend the tomatoes with water and set aside. Heat 1 tablespoon of oil and sauté the onion and okra pods. Add asafoetida, fenugreek powder, and green chili; stir well, until okra pods are cooked. Add the juice from the tomato mixture, salt, turmeric, and jaggery. Boil for 1 minute and remove from heat. In a separate pan, cook mustard seeds in remaining oil until they sputter and add to mixture. Garnish with coriander leaves.

123. Sathya/Dal Curry

1 cup toovar dal or moong dal
1/2 cup chopped tomatoes
1/2 jalapeno chili, slit
1 tsp. jaggery
1 tsp. turmeric powder
a pinch of asafoetida

2 tbs. oil
1/2 tsp. black mustard seeds
3 cups water
1 tbs. coriander leaves,
   chopped
1 tsp. salt

Cook dal with water in a pressure cooker for 3 minutes after bringing to maximum pressure. Allow to cool, then remove lid and lightly mash dal. Heat oil in a separate pan and cook mustard seeds until they sputter. Add tomatoes, salt, green chili, turmeric, asafoetida, and jaggery; cook until tomatoes are soft. Add this mixture to the dal and simmer for a minute. Garnish with coriander leaves.

124. Shakti/Potato Curry

4 large potatoes
1/2 tsp. turmeric powder

1/2 jalapeno chili, chopped
1 tsp. coriander powder

1 tsp. cumin powder 1 tbs. grated coconut
1/2 tsp. black mustard seeds 1 tsp. salt
1 tbs. jaggery 2 tbs. oil
4 cups water

Cook whole potatoes with water in a pressure cooker for 5 minutes after bringing to maximum pressure. Set cooking water aside. When cool remove lid; peel and cube potatoes. In a separate pan, heat oil and cook mustard seeds until they sputter. Add potatoes, coriander, turmeric, and cumin and stir-fry 1/2 minute. Stir in 2 cups of reserve water, salt, and jalapeno. Simmer for 3 minutes, add jaggery, and garnish with coconut.

125. Shastra/Mixed Dal Curry

1/2 cup toovar dal 2 tsp. cumin powder
1/4 cup lentils 1 jalapeno chili, chopped
1/4 cup green gram dal, skinned 1 tsp. fenugreek powder
1/2 cup split chickpeas 2 tbs. chopped mint leaves
2 onions, chopped 2 tsp. turmeric powder
1 cup chopped tomatoes 5 cups water
1 cup ripe pumpkin, cubed 1/4 tsp. asafoetida
1 cup potatoes, cubed 1 tbs. oil
1/2 cup eggplant, cubed 3 tsp. salt
1 tsp. black pepper powder 1 tbs. grated ginger
2 tsp. coriander powder

Soak chickpeas in water for 5 hours. Place chickpeas, lentils, green gram dal, and toovar dal in a pressure cooker. Add all vegetables, except tomato and 1 onion. Add 5 cups water, cover, and bring to maximum pressure. Reduce heat and cook for 15 minutes. Allow to cool and put mixture through a blender.

In a separate pan, heat oil and sauté the remaining onion. Add black pepper, coriander, cumin, chili, ginger, fenugreek, asafoetida, turmeric, and salt. Sauté for 2 minutes. Then add the blended vegetable-dal mix. Stir well and garnish with chopped mint leaves.

126. Sadhu/Lentil Curry

1/2 cup lentils	3 cups water
1/2 cup chopped carrots	1 tbs. lemon juice
1/4 cup chopped green beans	1/2 tsp. black mustard seeds
1/4 cup pumpkin, cubed	1 tsp. salt
1/2 tsp. turmeric powder	1 tbs. oil
1 tsp. grated ginger	1 tbs. chopped coriander leaves
1 jalapeno chili, chopped	

Clean and wash lentils and cook with 3 cups water in a pressure cooker for 3 minutes after bringing to maximum pressure. Remove lid and add vegetables, ginger, turmeric, chili, and salt; cook until vegetables are done. Heat oil in a frying pan and cook mustard seeds until they sputter. Add to curry, along with lemon juice, for seasoning. Garnish dish with coriander leaves.

127. Siddhi/Chickpea Curry

1 cup chickpeas	2 bay leaves
1/2 cup grated coconut	2 tbs. grated ginger
1/2 tsp. turmeric powder	1 jalapeno chili, chopped
1/2 tsp. cumin powder	1 tbs. jaggery
4 pieces cinnamon, 1/2" each	2 tbs. oil
3 cloves	1 tsp. salt
1 black cardamom pod	3-1/2 cups water

Wash and soak chickpeas in water to cover overnight. The next day, rinse the chickpeas and set aside. Heat the oil in a pressure cooker and fry ginger, chili, and all masala ingredients, except for the coconut, for 3 minutes uncovered. Add chickpeas and 3-1/2 cups water and bring to maximum pressure. Reduce heat and cook for 15 minutes Remove from heat and allow to cool. In the meantime, roast grated coconut in a frying pan without oil until brown. When the pressure cooker has cooled, remove lid and add salt, jaggery, and roasted coconut. Stir well.

128. Shraddha/Potato Surprise

4 large potatoes	1/4 tsp. cumin seeds
1/2 tsp. turmeric powder	1 tsp. grated ginger
1 tsp. coriander powder	2 tbs. chopped coriander leaves
1 tsp. cumin powder	3 cups water
1/2 jalapeno chili, chopped	2 tsp. salt
1 cup yogurt	1 tsp. oil

Cook potatoes with 2 cups of water in a pressure cooker for 5 minutes after bringing to maximum pressure. Remove from heat and allow to cool before removing lid. Peel and cube potatoes. Mix the yogurt with all the powders, green chili, and salt, and pour over potatoes. Heat oil in a pan and brown cumin seeds and ginger. Add to potato-yogurt mixture and stir. Mix in 1 cup of water and simmer for 3 minutes, uncovered. Garnish with coriander.

129. Swadharma/Vegetable Spicy Curry

3 cups mixed vegetables (carrots, turnips, green peas, cauliflower)	2 ripe tomatoes, chopped
	1/2 cup yogurt

82

1 tbs. lemon juice
1 tsp. oil

Masala
1 cup grated coconut
1/2 onion, chopped
2 jalapeno chilies, chopped
3 black cardamom pods

2 tsp. salt
3 cups water
1/2 onion, chopped

5 cloves
2 pieces cinnamon, 1" each
1 tsp. ginger, grated

Grind masala ingredients in an electric blender and set aside.

Wash and cut the vegetables (except tomatoes) and cook with 1 cups of water in a pressure cooker for 1 minute after bringing to maximum pressure. Mix the ground masala with the yogurt. In a separate pan, heat the oil and sauté onion. Add tomatoes and stir for 2 minutes. Mix in cooked vegetables, salt, and lemon juice. Add ground ingredients and mix well. Bring to a boil and remove from the heat. Garnish with coriander leaves.

130. Sudarshan/Green Peas and Paneer
1-1/2 cups freshly shelled green peas
1 cup chopped tomatoes
1 cup cubed paneer
1/2 tsp. red chili powder
1/2 tsp. turmeric powder
1 tsp. coriander powder
1 tsp. cumin powder

1 tsp. grated ginger
2 cups water
1/4 cup grated onions
2 tbs. chopped coriander
   leaves
1 tbs. oil
1 tsp. salt

Heat oil in a pressure cooker and sauté the onions until lightly brown. Add the ginger, tomatoes, and balance of the spices and sauté for 5 minutes. Stir continually until ingredients are well blended. Add green peas and sauté for another 2 minutes. Add water and cover; pressure

The foods that are stale, devoid of good taste, foul smelling, rotten, and impure are liked by those who are tamasic in nature.

—Bhagavad Gita,
Chapter 17, verse 10

cook for 1 minute after bringing to maximum pressure. When cool, remove lid and add paneer cubes. Simmer for a minute, uncovered. Garnish with fresh coriander leaves.

The vegetarian diet consisting of vegetables, eaten in normal quantity, provides a peaceful, healthy, and happy long life up to one's old age.

—PLATO

131. Sampoorna/Spinach Paneer

3 cups fresh spinach *(palak)*, chopped
1 cup cubed paneer
1/2 cup chopped tomatoes
1 onion, chopped
1 jalapeno chili, chopped
1/2 tbs. grated ginger

1 tsp. fenugreek leaves (or a pinch of fenugreek powder)
1 cup water
2 tbs. oil
1 tsp. salt

Sauté paneer in 1 tbs. oil, drain, and set aside. Cook spinach and fenugreek leaves in water. Remove greens from the heat and pass through a blender. Heat remaining oil in a separate pan and sauté the onions and ginger. Add tomatoes and mash well with a spoon. Add spinach mixture, jalapeno, salt, and fenugreek powder, if leaves are not available; mix well. Stir in paneer cubes and simmer for 3 minutes uncovered.

132. Shanti/Potatoes and Peas

1/2 cup freshly shelled green peas *(matar)*
1 cup cubed potatoes *(aloo)*
2 onions, grated
1/2 cup yogurt or chopped tomatoes
1 tsp. coriander powder
1 tsp. cumin powder

1/2 tsp. turmeric powder
1 tbs. grated ginger
1 jalapeno chili, minced
2 tsp. oil
2 cups water
1 tsp. salt

Cook potatoes and peas in water and set aside. Keep the cooking water. Heat oil in a separate pan and sauté the onions until soft. Add the ginger, then the yogurt or tomatoes, stirring continuously until ingredients are well mixed. Add the masala powders and green chili, and stir for another minute. Stir in salt and cooked vegetables with their cooking water; mix thoroughly and simmer uncovered for 3 minutes. Serve garnished with coriander leaves.

133. Samba/Moong Dal-Squash Curry

1/2 cup split moong dal (with skins)	1 tsp. turmeric powder
1 cup ash gourd, pumpkin, or other squash	1 tsp. cumin powder
	1 tsp. jaggery
2 cups of water	2 tbs. oil
1 cup chopped tomatoes	1 small jalapeno chili, minced
1 onion, chopped	
1 tsp. grated ginger	1 tsp. salt

Cook dal and squash with water in a pressure cooker for 3 minutes after bringing to maximum pressure. Heat oil in a separate pan and sauté onions. Add the minced chili, ginger, turmeric and cumin powders and sauté for 2 minutes. Mix in tomatoes and stir until soft. Mash lightly. Stir in salt, jaggery, and cooked vegetable-dal. Mix well and sprinkle with coriander leaves.

Koftas are deep-fried vegetable balls.

134. Samarpan/Kofta Curry

2 potatoes, boiled	1 tbs. minced onion
1 carrot, grated	1 tbs. fresh corn meal
1 small beetroot, grated	3 tomatoes, chopped
1/2 cup oil	1 small onion, minced
1 tsp. garam masala (see p. 23)	1 tsp. jaggery
1 tbs. chopped coriander leaves	1 tsp. salt

1 tsp. turmeric powder
1 tsp. cumin powder

2 tbs. coriander leaves
2 cups water

Put tomatoes through a blender and set aside. Grate carrots and beetroot; peel and mash potatoes. Add garam masala, minced onion, chopped coriander, and corn meal to the grated and mashed vegetables. Mix well and make into 5 or 6 balls. To make firmer balls, add more corn meal. Heat oil and deep fry balls, draining them on a paper towel.

Heat a little of the oil in which the balls have been fried in a separate pan and sauté the onions. Add the cumin, turmeric powder, salt, and jaggery. Finally, add the blended tomatoes and water and simmer a few minutes. About 10 minutes before serving, slip the vegetable balls gently into the gravy and sprinkle with fresh coriander leaves.

135. Sadhaka/Dried Chickpea Curry

1 cup whole chickpeas (chana)
   soaked overnight in 2 cups water
1 cup chopped tomatoes
2 tbs. coriander powder
2 tbs. cumin powder
1 tsp. garam masala (see p. 23)
1 tbs. grated ginger

1 jalapeno chili, minced
2 tbs. oil
1 onion, chopped
1 tsp. salt
3 cups water
1 tbs. lemon juice
1/2 cup minced coriander leaves

Soak the chickpeas in enough water to come 3/4" above the peas. In the morning, rinse chickpeas and cook in a pressure cooker with 3 cups of water for 15 minutes on low heat after bringing to maximum pressure. Set aside to cool before uncovering.

Heat oil in a separate pan and sauté onion, ginger, and green chili for 3 minutes. Add coriander and cumin powders and sauté another minute. Stir in cooked chickpeas with a little of their cooking water. Blend well and simmer for 5 minutes uncovered, adding more water if necessary. Add salt, lemon juice, garam masala, and garnish with minced coriander leaves.

136. Shree/Red Pinto Bean Curry

1 cup red pinto beans *(rajma)*
1/2 cup grated onions
1/2 cup chopped tomatoes
1 tbs. grated ginger
1 tsp. garam masala (see p. 23)
1 jalapeno chili, minced

1 tsp. salt
2 tsp. jaggery
2 tbs. oil
3 cups water
1/2 cup fresh coriander leaves, chopped

Soak beans overnight in 4 cups of water. Heat oil in a pressure cooker and sauté the onion. Add ginger, jaggery, and tomatoes and sauté until well blended. Rinse beans and add them, along with 3 cups of water, the green chili, and salt, to the tomato mixture. Cover pressure cooker and bring to maximum pressure. Reduce heat and cook for 25 minutes. Remove from heat and allow to cool before uncovering. Add garam masala and garnish with fresh coriander leaves.

137. Sharanam/Chana-Kurma or Spicy Chickpeas

1 cup chickpeas, washed
1/2 cup cubed paneer
2 onions, grated
1/2 cup chopped tomatoes
1 tbs. grated ginger
1 tbs. chopped coriander leaves
2 tbs. oil
1 tsp. salt

3 cups water
2 black cardamom pods
2 pieces cinnamon, 1" each
4 cloves
2 bay leaves
1/2 tsp. turmeric powder
1 tbs. ghee

Wash and soak beans overnight. The next day, drain beans and discard water. Heat oil in a pressure cooker and sauté the onions. Add ginger, cinnamon, cloves, cardamom pods, and bay leaves. Sauté for 2 minutes, add tomatoes, and cook. Lightly mash with ladle until well blended. Mix in soaked beans, salt, turmeric, and sauté for another minute. Add 3 cups water and cover. Cook and bring to maximum pressure. Reduce heat and cook for 15 minutes. In a separate pan, heat ghee and lightly sauté paneer cubes. When cooker cools, remove lid and add lightly fried paneer cubes. Simmer for another 2 minutes.

Chapter Twelve: Vishveshwara Woked Vegetables

Vegetables should be eaten raw whenever possible; when they have to be cooked, this should be done in a minimum of water. The cooking water should not be thrown away but utilized in soups and gravies. More nutritional value is retained if vegetables are steamed. Another good method of cooking them is in a Chinese or Indian wok, with little or no water. The wok should be moistened with a little oil and covered with a tight-fitting lid. The heat should be kept to a minimum so that moisture forms on the lid and the vegetables cook in their own juices. This method retains maximum flavor. Almost any vegetable can be cooked in this way.

138. Tejas/Sprouted Lentils (Serves 4)

2 cups fresh moong or lentil sprouts
a pinch of asafoetida
1/2 tsp. turmeric powder
1 jalapeno chili, minced
1 tsp. grated ginger

2 tbs. grated coconut
1 small onion, minced
1 tbs. oil
1/2 tsp. salt

Heat oil in a wok and sauté the onion until soft. Add ginger and sauté for a minute; mix in asafoetida, green chili, turmeric, and salt. Sauté for a while longer, then add sprouted beans and sauté a few more minutes. Cover and cook for 1 minute on low heat. Remove from heat and serve with grated coconut.

139. Ojas/French Beans Sauté (Serves 4)

2 cups french beans, cut fine	1 onion, minced
1/4 tsp. aniseed	1/2 tsp. salt
1 jalapeno chili, minced	1 tbs. oil
1 tsp. grated ginger	

Heat oil in a wok and sauté the onion. Add green chili, ginger, and aniseed and sauté for another minute. Add beans and stir. Cover and cook for 3 minutes on low heat. Uncover and stir occasionally, until water evaporates and beans are cooked.

140. Ananta/Cabbage Sauté (Serves 4)

2 cups shredded cabbage	1 tbs. oil
1 cup grated carrots	1/2 tsp. salt
1 onion, chopped	2 tbs. grated coconut
1 tsp. black mustard seeds	

Heat oil in a wok and cook mustard seeds until they sputter. Add onion and sauté until soft. Add cabbage, carrots, and salt. Cover and cook for 3 minutes. Uncover and stir for another few minutes, until water evaporates. Garnish with grated coconut.

The foods that promote life, mental strength, vitality, health, cheerfulness, and a loving nature, that are savory, nutritious, digestible and agreeable, these are dear to the sattvic nature.

—BHAGAVAD GITA,
CHAPTER 17, VERSE 8

141. Turiya/Okra Sauté (Serves 4 to 6)

3 cups okra, chopped in 1/2" pieces	1/2 tsp. salt
1/2 cup chopped tomatoes	3 tbs. oil
1 onion, chopped	1 tbs. chopped coriander
1/2 tsp. grated ginger	leaves

Heat oil in a wok and sauté onion lightly. Add ginger and sauté for a minute. Add okra pods and salt and stir for 5 more minutes. Then add chopped tomatoes and keep stirring until all ingredients are well mixed and cooked. Garnish with coriander leaves and serve.

142. Tapovan/Spinach Sauté (Serves 4 to 6)

6 cups fresh spinach, chopped	1 tbs. oil
1 onion, chopped	1/2 tsp. salt
1/2 tsp. cumin powder	1 tbs. grated coconut

Heat oil in a wok and sauté the onions. Add cumin and sauté, then add spinach and salt. Cover well and cook for 3 minutes on low heat. Uncover, stir, and cover again. Repeat until spinach is soft and cooked. Garnish with grated coconut.

143. Anaadi/Spicy Spinach Sauté (Serves 4 to 6)

6 cups fresh spinach, chopped	1/2 tsp. black mustard seeds
2 tbs. minced onion	1/2 tsp. salt
1/2 cup boiled peanuts	1 jalapeno chili, minced
1/2 tsp. cumin powder	1/2 tsp. turmeric powder
a pinch of asafoetida	2 tbs. oil
1 tomato, chopped	1/2 cup water

Boil peanuts in unsalted water for 5 minutes; drain and set aside. Cook spinach in 1/2 cup water, blend with a fork, and set aside. Heat oil in a wok and cook mustard seeds until they sputter; add onions and sauté. Add cumin and asafoetida and stir. Mix in green chili and tomato and sauté well, until tomato becomes soft. Stir in turmeric powder, salt, and the mashed spinach. Finally, add the boiled peanuts.

144. Uttama/Whole Okra Sauté (Serves 2)

10-12 small, tender okra pods	1 tsp. salt
1/2 tsp. coriander powder	4 tbs. oil
1 tsp. cumin powder	1 tomato, sliced
1 tsp. turmeric powder	2 tbs. chopped coriander leaves

Wash and dry okra pods and slit each one once on the side, taking care not to slit the complete length; do not chop off the tops. Mix all powders and salt together and stuff mixture into the slits. Heat oil in a wok and place okra pods side-by-side. Sauté on low heat, turning over gently so that all sides are cooked. Garnish with tomato slices and coriander leaves and serve.

145. Vairagya/Mashed Eggplant (Serves 2)

1 large eggplant	1/2 tsp. turmeric powder
1 onion, chopped	a pinch of asafoetida
3 ripe tomatoes, chopped	1 tsp. salt
1 jalapeno chili, minced	1 tbs. oil
1 tsp. coriander powder	2 tbs. chopped coriander leaves

Coat the eggplant lightly with oil and roast at moderate heat, either on hot coals or under the broiler, until the skin becomes loose. Remove skin and chop eggplant into small pieces. Heat oil in a wok and sauté onions; add green chili and tomatoes and sauté until well cooked. Mix in eggplant and keep stirring and mashing with a spoon until well blended. Add salt, turmeric powder, coriander powder, and asafoetida. Stir and cook for 3 minutes. Garnish with coriander leaves.

146. Vedanta/Stuffed Eggplant (Serves 4 to 6)

6 small, roundish eggplants
2 ripe tomatoes
2 tsp. freshly grated coconut
2 tsp. coriander powder
2 tsp. cumin powder
1/2 tsp. turmeric powder
2 tsp. jaggery

1 tbs. grated ginger
1/2 cup water
4 tbs. oil
2 tsp. salt
1/2 cup chopped coriander
   leaves

Wash and make 4 slits lengthwise in each eggplant, but do not slice through; slits should go only up to stalk. Grind coconut and ginger powders together in an electric grinder; mix salt, and sugar together. Stuff the eggplants with this masala. Any remaining masala may be set aside. Heat oil in a wok and cook stuffed eggplants gently, turning them until the color changes. Then add the tomatoes, water, and remaining spices (if any) and cover with tight-fitting lid. Cook for 5 minutes on low. Uncover and stir gently, so as not to break eggplants. Remove from heat when cooked and garnish with coriander leaves.

147. Veda/Whole Potato Sauté (Serves 4 to 6)

10 small potatoes
1 onion, chopped
1 tomato, chopped
1/2 tsp. turmeric powder

1/4 tsp. cumin seeds
1/4 tsp. garam masala (see p. 23)
1 tsp. grated ginger
1 tbs. oil

2-1/2 cup water   2 tbs. coriander leaves
2 tsp. salt

Boil potatoes in water with their jackets. When cool, peel and set
aside. Heat oil in a wok and sauté cumin seeds. Cook for a minute
then add onions and sauté until brown. Add turmeric, salt, ginger,
and mix. Lastly add potatoes. Stir well, blend in tomato, and cover
with a tight-gitting lid. Cook for 3 minutes until all the liquid
evaporates. Mix in garam masala and garnish with coriander leaves.

148. Vibhuti/Potato Yogurt (Serves 4 to 6)
10 small potatoes   3 tbs. oil
4 tbs. yogurt   2 tsp. salt
1/2 tsp. turmeric powder   2 cups water
2 tsp. coriander powder   black pepper powder to taste
2 tsp. cumin powder

Boil potatoes in water with their jackets. When cool, peel, prick
with a fork, and set aside. Heat oil in a wok. Mix powders and salt
in yogurt and spread evenly over the potatoes. Put potatoes into
heated oil and stir-fry until all liquid is absorbed and potatoes are a
golden brown. Sprinkle with black pepper and serve.

149. Viveka/Spicy Carrots (Serves 2)
1 cup carrots, cut into cubes   1/4 cup water
1/2 cup peas, shelled   1 tbs. oil
1/2 tsp. turmeric powder   1 onion, chopped
1/2 tsp. black pepper powder   1 tsp. salt
1/2 tsp. grated ginger

Heat oil and sauté the onion. Add carrots and peas and sauté for 2 minutes. Lower heat; add ginger, turmeric, and salt and stir for a few minutes. Add water and cover. Cook on low for 5 minutes until water is almost gone. Uncover and keep stirring until all liquid is absorbed. Sprinkle with black pepper.

150. Yajna/Spicy Pumpkin (Serves 2 to 4)

2 cups pumpkin, cubed	1 tsp. salt
1 onion, chopped	2 tbs. oil
1/4 tsp. fenugreek seeds	1/2 cup water
1/2 tsp. turmeric powder	1/2 tsp. black mustard seeds
1/2 tsp. red chili powder	a pinch of asafoetida

Heat oil in a wok and cook mustard seeds until they sputter. Add fenugreek seeds and asafoetida and stir for a minute. Sauté onion until soft. Add turmeric, chili, and salt and mix well. Blend in pumpkin cubes and stir for another 2 minutes. Add water, cover, and cook on low heat for 5 minutes. Uncover, stir, and cover again. Continue this process until all water is absorbed.

151. Yuga/Sautéed Moong Dal (Serves 4 to 6)

1 cup split moong dal, with skins	1 tbs. oil
1 onion, chopped	1 tsp. salt
1/2 tsp. cumin seeds	1-1/4 cup water
1/2 tbs. grated ginger	1 jalapeno chili, minced
1/2 tsp. turmeric powder	2 tbs. coriander leaves, chopped
2 tsp. lemon juice	

Cook dal in a pressure cooker for 3 minutes after bringing to maximum pressure; allow to cool before removing lid. Heat oil in a wok and sauté the onion. Add cumin seeds, ginger, green chili, salt, and turmeric powder. Mix in cooked dal and stir well, until water evaporates. Add lemon juice and garnish with coriander leaves.

152. Nirvana/Spicy Mushrooms (Serves 4 to 6)

2 cups chopped mushrooms
1 onion, chopped
1/2 tsp. garam masala (see p. 23)
1/4 cup water
1 tbs. ghee
1/4 tsp. turmeric powder
salt to taste

Heat ghee in a wok and sauté onions. Add chopped mushrooms and sauté for 2 minutes. Add turmeric and water, cover with tight-fitting lid, and cook for 5 minutes on medium heat. Uncover and stir-fry until water is completely absorbed. Lastly, add garam masala and serve hot on toast or as a side dish.

153. Brahmin/Chinese Eggplant (Serves 4)

2 medium-sized eggplants, cut in
   1/2" strips
1/2 tsp. minced ginger
1 jalapeno chili, minced
3 tbs. oil
1/2 tsp. mustard powder
a few springs of Chinese
   parsley

Sauce

1/2 cup water
1 tbs. jaggery
1 tbs. cornstarch
1 tbs. sesame oil (not dark)
2 tsp. lemon juice
1 tbs. soya sauce
salt to taste

Heat oil in a wok. Add ginger, green chili, and mustard powder. Stir a few minutes, add eggplant, and stir-fry until cooked. In a small bowl, combine all ingredients for the sauce. Add sauce to the eggplant and stir for a few minutes. Garnish with Chinese parsley.

Chapter Thirteen: Poornanand Sweets & Desserts

In India, as in most countries, a sweet dish to follow a meal is a must. Most traditional Indian sweets are rather heavy since they contain a lot of ghee and milk. They are not suitable for those who follow a Nature Care diet. The dishes given below are both tasty and nutritive, as well as easy to make, unlike the traditional sweets.

154. Krishnamrit/Carrot Dessert (Serves 4 to 6)

2 cups grated carrot
1/2 cup sago (washed) or tapioca pearls
1 quart fresh cow's milk
1 cup jaggery
2 tbs. raisins

2 tbs. chopped almonds or cashews
1 tsp. vanilla extract
2 tbs. ghee

Soak sago pearls in 2 cups of water for 1/2 and hour. Heat the ghee in a heavy-bottomed pan. Lightly sauté raisins and cashews and set aside. (If almonds are used, they should be blanched, peeled, and chopped instead of sautéed.) In the remaining ghee, lightly sauté the grated carrots for about 3 minutes. Add milk and sago pearls. Bring to a boil and continue stirring until mixture comes to a rolling boil. Lower heat and simmer for 15 minutes, until milk starts to thicken. Keep stirring occasionally, then add the nuts and raisins. Remove from heat. Add jaggery and stir well. Mix in vanilla extract. This sweet can be served either hot or cold. It will keep for a couple of days in the refrigerator.

155. Krishnanand/Fruit Cream (Serves 4)

2 bananas, sliced
2 apples, chopped
1/4 cup raisins
1/4 cup freshly grated coconut
1 orange, peeled and chopped
1 pear, chopped
1 cup chopped pineapple
4 cups yogurt
1/4 cup chopped nuts and dates

Blend the yogurt with all the fruits until creamy. Pour into individual dishes and chill. Top with nuts and dates before serving.

156. Aja/Fruit Frolic (Serves 2)

1 mango (or any pulpy fruit)
1 cup yogurt
a pinch of green cardamom
1 tbs. crushed nuts

Chop fruit and put with yogurt and cardamom powder through a blender. Mix in nuts and chill well before serving.

157. Aishwarya/Rice Pudding (Serves 4 to 6)

6 cups milk
3/4 cup rice
1/2 cup raisins
1/4 tsp. green cardamom powder
1/2 bay leaf
2 cups jaggery

Cook rice with milk and bay leaf. Bring to a boil and reduce heat. Simmer for 40 minutes until rice starts to thicken, stirring often. Remove bay leaf and add jaggery, raisins, and cardamom powder. Serve either hot or cold.

158. Achintya/Brown Rice Delight (Serves 4 to 6)

1 cup brown rice
1 cup jaggery
2 tbs. cashews
1 tbs. raisins

Doctor, no medicine. We are machines made to live—organized especially for this purpose. Such is our nature. Do not counter-act the living principle. Leave it at liberty to defend itself and it will do better than your drugs.

—NAPOLEON

97

6 green cardamom pods, crushed   2-1/2 cups water
4 tbs. ghee

Dissolve jaggery in 1 cup of water, strain, and set aside. Heat 1 tablespoon of ghee in pressure cooker, add rice, and sauté for a few minutes. Stir in 1-1/2 cup water, cover, and bring to full pressure. Reduce heat and cook for 5 minutes. Remove from heat and allow to cool before uncovering. Add dissolved sugar mixture and 2 tablespoons of ghee. Return to heat and keep stirring until all water is absorbed. Sauté cashews and raisins separately in remaining tablespoon of ghee and add to rice mixture. Add crushed cardamom, mix, and serve.

159. Sanathana/Moong Dal Pudding (Serves 6)
1 cup moong dal   2 cups coconut milk, thick
1 cup jaggery   1 tsp. green cardamom
2 cups coconut milk, thin   1 tbs. ghee

Heat ghee and sauté moong dal for 3 minutes. Add 2 cups of thin coconut milk and cook until dal is soft. Add jaggery and stir until dissolved. Add 2 cups of thick coconut milk and cardamom powder. Stir well and heat, but do not boil. Serve either hot or cold.

160. Krishnapriya/Papaya Pleasure (Serves 4 to 6)
1 small ripe papaya   4 cups fresh coconut milk
4 ripe bananas   1/4 cup chopped cashews
1/2 cup honey   2 tsp. green cardamom powder
1/2 cup chopped dates

Chop fruit and blend with honey and coconut milk. Add cashews, dates, and cardamom powder. Chill and serve.

161. Vaikund/Nut Yogurt (Serves 4)

2 cups yogurt
2 tbs. honey
4 tbs. ground almonds
1 tbs. chopped nuts
a few cherries for decoration

Blend yogurt, almonds, and honey together. Fill individual dessert bowls with the mixture. Decorate with chopped nuts and cherries. Chill before serving.

162. Vyasa/Yogurt Jelly (Serves 4 to 6)

2 cups yogurt
1/2 cup fresh fruit juice (any kind)
1/2 cup fresh fruit pieces
2 tbs. honey
2 tbs. agar-agar flakes
1/2 cup warm water

Boil water and dissolve agar in it. Blend yogurt, fruit juice, and honey. Add dissolved agar flakes and blend again. Pour into individual glasses and cool. Decorate with fruit pieces.

163. Surya Narayana/Coconut Jelly (Serves 4)

1/2 cup unroasted cashews, coarsely ground
2 cups water
1 tbs. agar-agar flakes
1/4 cup honey
1/4 tsp. salt
1/2 cup freshly grated coconut
1 tsp. vanilla extract

Mix cashews and water in a pan. Add agar flakes and boil until they dissolve. Slowly stir in all other ingredients, except the honey. Cook over low heat, stirring constantly. Remove from heat, add honey, and pour into separate bowls. Cool until set and serve.

164. Swami/Coconut Candy (Serves 6)

4 cups milk

1/2 cup heavy cream

1 cup jaggery

1/2 cup freshly grated coconut

1 tsp. vanilla extract

Boil milk and cream over high heat, stirring to prevent sticking. Reduce heat when milk starts to boil. Continue to cook on low heat; it will begin to thicken after half an hour. Stir milk until a small amount dropped into cold water forms a small soft ball. Add jaggery, coconut, and vanilla and stir well. Pour onto a flat buttered tray. When cool cut into desired shapes, and allow to harden. This candy will keep for a week refrigerated.

165. Shauri/Coconut Milk Fudge (Serves 4 to 6)

1/4 cup ghee

1/4 cup jaggery

3/4 cup freshly grated coconut

3/4 cup whole dry milk powder

1 tsp. green cardamom powder

1/2 tsp. nutmeg

Melt ghee and jaggery over medium heat. Stir in milk powder, coconut, cardamom, and nutmeg. Press mixture into a lightly buttered tray. Refrigerate until hard. Cut into desired shapes and serve.

166. Upanishad/Dried Fruit Jelly (Serves 4)

1 cup dates, minced

1 cup raisins, minced

1 cup figs, minced

1 cup fruit juice

2 tbs. agar-agar flakes

1 tbs. honey

Boil agar and fruit juice in a pan until agar dissolves. Remove from heat, add honey, and stir. Stir minced dry fruits into mixture. Pour into a tray and refrigerate. When firm, cut into squares.

167. Ramana/Raisin Balls (Makes 20 to 25 Balls)

2-1/2 cups raisins   1 cup freshly grated coconut

Mince raisins. Shape raisins into balls and roll in grated coconut. Refrigerate to harden and serve.

168. Mahalakshmi/Almond Balls (Makes 25 to 30 Balls)

2-1/2 cups almonds   1/2 cup honey

Put almonds through an electric grinder. Set 1/2 cup of ground almonds aside and mix the rest with honey to form a thick paste. Make small balls and roll in ground nuts. Refrigerate to harden.

169. Jagannath/Date-Nut Balls (Makes 20 to 25 Balls)

1 cup raw peanuts, without skins   1/2 cup water
1-1/4 cups dates, minced

Put raw peanuts through a blender. Remove 2 tablespoons of ground nuts and set aside. To remaining nuts in blender, add water slowly and blend to make peanut butter. Remove from blender and combine with minced dates. Roll mixture into balls 1/2" thick and refrigerate to harden. Cut into pieces and top with remaining ground nuts.

170. Shriniketan/Stuffed Dates (Makes 10 to 15 Balls)

2-1/2 cups dates   2 tbs. honey
1 cup ground peanuts

Carefully remove pits from dates by slitting open one side. Combine ground peanuts with honey. Insert mixture into dates and close well by pressing the sides together. Chill before serving.

171. Keertan/Dried Fruit-Coconut Balls (Makes 20 to 30 Balls)

2-1/2 cups prunes

2-1/2 cups dates

1/2 cup walnut meat, chopped

1 cup freshly grated coconut

Remove pits from prunes and dates and put flesh through a mincer. Add chopped nuts. Roll mixture into small balls and coat with fresh coconut. Refrigerate to harden.

172. Deenadayal/Fruit-Nut Pie (Serves 4 to 6)

Crust

1/4 cup sesame seeds

1/4 cup sunflower seeds

1/4 cup walnut meat

1 tbs. butter

1 tbs. honey

Grind sesame, sunflower, and walnuts very fine. Put mixture in a bowl, add butter, and fold together with a knife until well combined. Add honey and stir. Butter a pie dish and mold this crust into the center. With wet fingers, press crust evenly around the pie dish and up the sides. Refrigerate for an hour or more.

Filling

4 bananas, peeled and cut in rounds

4 apples, cored and quartered

1/2 cup figs or dates, chopped

1/2 tsp. cinnamon

1 tbs. lemon juice

1 cup finely ground walnut meat

Combine bananas, apples, and dried fruit. Mix in lemon juice and cinnamon. Pour into pie crust. Smooth surface and top with minced walnut meat. Refrigerate overnight or at least 4 hours before serving.

173. Shreekhand/Yogurt Cream (Serves 4 to 6)

5 cups fresh yogurt

2 cups finely powdered white sugar
  or confectioner's sugar

1 cup chopped cashews

1 tsp. green cardamom
  powder

The foods that augment life, energy, strength, health, happiness, and joy and that are savory, oleaginous, nourishing, and agreeable are liked by the sattvika.

—BHAGAVAD GITA
CHAPTER 17, VERSE 8

Suspend yogurt in a cheesecloth bag for an hour or so, until all the water drains off. Remove yogurt and combine with the sugar and cardamom, either by hand or with a blender, until smooth. Put in individual bowls and sprinkle with chopped cashews. Serve cold.

The dishes selected here are those especially favored by guests at Vanamali. They do not fit within the framework of purely Natural Cooking, since many of these dishes are fried and we normally do not encourage the eating of fried foods. On "special ocassions," however, a little indulgence is excusable. So enjoy!

174. Amala/Savory Doughnuts (Serves 4 to 6)

1 cup split black gram, preferably with skin
1/2 cup grated carrot
3 tbs. freshly grated coconut
5 cups yogurt
1 bunch coriander leaves, chopped
salt and pepper to taste
2 cups oil
red chili powder to taste

Soak black gram overnight. In the morning, wash well and remove loose skins. Drain water and grind gram fairly coarsely in an electric grinder. Do not add water while grinding. Add grated carrot, coconut, and coriander leaves to the batter, which should be quite thick. Beat yogurt until smooth; add salt, a little pepper, and coriander leaves. Mix well and set aside.

Heat oil in a frying pan. Lightly oil the palm of your hand. Pour one tablespoon of the batter into your palm, flatten slightly, and slide it carefully into the boiling oil.

Two or 3 doughnuts can be put into the oil at the same time. Turn each doughnut over when it becomes golden brown.

Chapter Fourteen: Vanamali Special Dishes

As doughnuts are taken out of the oil, drain well and drop them into the yogurt mixture. Repeat process until no batter remains. Allow to set for a few hours, until the doughnuts soak up the yogurt. Sprinkle freshly cut coriander leaves and red chili powder on top.

175. Janardan/Eggplant Delight (Serves 4 to 6)

2 large eggplants, sliced lengthwise in 1/4" strips	a pinch of asafoetida or fenugreek powder
1 large onion, thinly sliced	2 tbs. chopped coriander leaves
2 cups yogurt	1/2 tsp. turmeric powder
1 jalapeno chili, chopped	salt to taste
1 tsp. freshly grated ginger	2 tbs. oil

Slice eggplants and onions; cut onion slices in half. In a bowl, beat yogurt with a fork. Mix in salt and chopped coriander, and set aside.

Heat oil and sauté onions and eggplants until soft, stirring occasionally to prevent burning. Add asafoetida or fenugreek powder, ginger, green chili, and turmeric powder. Stir for 2 minutes and remove from heat. Combine with yogurt mixture. Chill and serve, sprinkled with coriander leaves.

176. Leela/Vegetable Omlette (Serves 4)

6 medium-sized potatoes	2 tbs. chopped coriander leaves
1/4 cup chickpea flour (besan)	
1/2 cup onion, thinly sliced	1/2 tsp. garam masala (see p. 23)
2 large tomatoes, chopped	salt and pepper to taste
1/2 cup grated carrot	1/2 tsp. turmeric powder
1/2 cup grated paneer (see p. 20)	4-1/2 tbs. oil

Health, that precious heritage, of priest and layman, fool and sage. It's worth a hundred times its cost, but no one learns that, until it is lost.

—ANON

104

Peel and grate potatoes and put into a bowl. After 5 minutes, squeeze out liquid from potatoes and add salt, pepper, and chickpea flour. Mix and set aside. If there is still too much liquid in the bowl, add a little more flour.

In a frying pan, heat 1/2 tablespoon of oil and sauté the onions. Add carrots and sauté for another 5 minutes. Add tomatoes, coriander leaves, and garam masala. Stir well. Remove from heat and set aside.

In a heavy skillet, heat 1 tablespoon of oil and coat entire interior of skillet. Divide potato mixture into 4 parts. Take 1 portion and spread it evenly over the bottom of skillet. Cover and cook over low heat, until the potatoes are cooked and hold together. Flip the "omlette" over and cook until the bottom turns a golden brown. Flip again and cover half the omlette with a quarter of the filling; top with some of the grated paneer. Fold omlette in half. Press down and continue heating for a minute more. Transfer omlette to a plate and serve immediately. Repeat with the other 3 portions.

177. Mohan/Lentil Burgers (Serves 4 to 6)

1/2 cup lentils	1 tsp. garam masala (see p. 23)
1 cup water	1/2 cup chopped coriander
2 tbs. chopped onion	1 cup oil
1/2 cup grated carrot	1/2 tsp. black pepper powder
1 tomato, chopped	salt to taste
2 tbs. sesame seeds	4 tbs. tomato sauce
1/2 cup chickpea flour (besan)	1 large cucumber, sliced

Cook lentils in a pressure cooker with water and tomato for 3 minutes after bringing to maximum presssure. Remove from heat and allow to cool before uncovering. There should not be any water in the lentils; if there is, drain and keep liquid for soups. Mash ingredients well—consistency should be firm. Add onion, carrots, garam masala, sesame seeds, salt, pepper, and coriander leaves. Lastly, add flour and mix well to form 4 to 6 individual patties.

Heat oil in a skillet and sauté burgers on both sides until golden brown. As an alternative, these patties can also be baked at 450°F. for half an hour. Serve with slices of cucumber and some homemade tomato sauce.

178. Devadas/Cauliflower Fritters (Serves 4 to 6)

1 medium-sized cauliflower, large flowerettes
2 cups oil
1 cup chickpea flour (besan)
1 tsp. garam masala (see p. 23)
3 tbs. chopped coriander leaves
1 tsp. black pepper powder
salt to taste
1/2 cup water
4 tbs. tomato sauce or 1/2 cup coconut-mint chutney

Mix all ingredients, except oil, cauliflower, and sauce/chutney. Make a thick batter, adding water. Heat oil in a deep pan or wok. Dip cauliflower pieces in the batter and deep fry in the oil. Turn pieces until they brown on all sides. Drain excess oil on paper towels. Serve with tomato sauce or coconut-mint chutney.

179. Achyutha/Cauliflower-Nut Bites (Serves 4 to 6)

2 cups small cauliflower flowerettes
1/2 cup whole cashews
1 tsp. salt
2 cups oil
1/2 tsp. black pepper powder
4 tbs. tomato sauce or 1/4 cup tomato chutney

Heat oil in wok and deep fry flowerettes. Drain on paper towels and set aside. Place cashews in a small strainer and dip them into the oil for ten seconds. Remove and drain. Combine cauliflower and cashew and add salt and pepper by placing in a plastic bag and shaking. Serve with tomato sauce or tomato chutney.

180. Nitya/Vegetarian Tostadas (Serves 4)

2 tbs. whole wheat flour, finely powdered *(atta)*	5 tbs. water
2 tbs. fresh cornmeal	salt to taste

Combine all ingredients and make dough as for ordinary chapatis.

Filling

1 cup fresh mushrooms, chopped	1 tbs. oil
1/2 cup chopped onions	1 tsp. cumin powder
1 cup chopped tomatoes	1 tsp. black pepper powder
1 cup chopped green bell pepper	1 cup homemade tomato sauce
1/2 cup cucumber slices	1/4 cup green olives, pitted
1 cup crumbled paneer	(optional)

Sauté onions and mushrooms in oil until tender. Add cumin, pepper, and salt and stir well. Add pepper and tomatoes and cook for 2 minutes and divide filling into 4 portions.

Make 4 chapatis as usual on a *tawa* but toast them until they become crispy tostadas. Place each tostada on a separate plate and immediately layer equal amounts of the mushroom mixture, paneer, and cucumber. Top with tomato sauce and chopped olives. Serve hot.

Filling Variation

2 cups cooked red kidney beans *(rajma)*	1 tsp. red chili powder
1 cup grated Parmesan cheese	1/2 tsp. coriander powder
1 onion, chopped	1/2 tsp. cumin powder
2 tbs. ghee	2 tomatoes, sliced

1 cucumber, sliced   salt to taste
1/2 cup chopped coriander leaves

Heat ghee, and sauté onions. Add cumin powder and salt. Stir in cooked beans and mash thoroughly. Add coriander leaves and mix well. Spread this mixture on each tostada. Top with sliced tomatoes, cucumber, and cheese. Cover with tomato sauce and serve.

181. Poorna/Enchiladas (Serves 2 to 4)
1/2 cup whole wheat flour *(atta)*   1 cup water
1/2 cup corn meal flour   3 tsp. ghee

Combine all ingredients and make dough as for ordinary chapatis. Make 6 soft and pliable chapatis—enchiladas—on a *tawa*. Smear each one with 1/2 teaspoon of ghee so that they remain soft.

Filling
2 onions, minced   1/2 tsp. black pepper powder
2 cups fresh sweet corn   1/2 cup thick tomato sauce
2 cups fresh spinach, chopped   2 tsp. jaggery
1 cup sour cream or fresh yogurt   2 cups grated Cheddar cheese
1/2 tsp. coriander powder   2-1/2 tbs. oil
1/2 tsp. cumin powder   salt to taste

Heat 2 tablespoons oil in a frying pan and sauté onions. Add corn, coriander, cumin, salt and pepper and sauté. Add jaggery and spinach. Stir well for a minute, remove from heat, and blend in 1 cup of grated cheese. Divide mixture into 6 portions.

Place 1 portion of this filling in a strip down the center of each enchilada. When all 6 enchiladas are made, roll each one up. In a large oiled baking dish that is coated with tomato sauce, place 3 enchiladas, seam down. Make a second layer, with remaining 3 enchiladas. Cover again with sauce and sprinkle with the remaining cheese. Bake at 450°F. for 15 minutes. Remove from oven and cut into 3 or 4 pieces. Top each with a tablespoon of sour cream or yogurt and serve.

182. Devi/Semolina Savory (Serves 2 to 4)

1 cup semolina *(sooji)*	2 tbs. chopped coriander
1 cup grated carrots	2-1/4 cups water
1 onion, minced	5 tbs. ghee or oil
1 tsp. black mustard seeds	2 tsp. lemon juice
8 cashews, chopped	salt to taste
a pinch of asafoetida	

In a frying pan, fry semolina without oil until it becomes a light brown color. Remove and keep aside.

Heat ghee or oil in the same pan and cook mustard seeds until they sputter. Add cashews and fry a minute, then add the asafoetida. Mix in onion and sauté for a few minutes, then add carrots and sauté for 5 minutes. Now add water and salt. When water starts to boil vigorously, reduce heat and slowly add the semolina, stirring constantly to prevent lumping (add semolina with the left hand and stir with the right). Stir well until the water is absorbed, then cover and put on low heat for a few minutes. Uncover and stir again. Add chopped coriander and lemon juice and stir once more. The consistency should be soft and smooth, not sticky. Some types of semolina need less cooking, so the quantity of water should be adjusted accordingly.

183. Rama/Dosas or Rice-Dal Pancakes (Makes 20 to 25 Dosas)

2 cups rice	salt to taste
3/4 cup black gram dal (split)	1/2 cup sesame oil
2 tsp. fenugreek seeds	5 cups water

One who has controlled the sense of Taste can control all other senses.

—Srimad Bhagavad Purana

109

Soak the rice in 3 cups of water. In a separate bowl, soak the black gram dal with the fenugreek seeds in 2 cups of water. Leave both to soak overnight. In the morning, rinse well and drain the water but do not discard. Using a little of this dal water, grind the rice and gram separately until very fine). Mix together and add enough water to make a fairly thick and smooth batter that flows smoothly when poured. Add salt and set aside to allow batter to ferment slightly for 4 to 8 hours. (Length of time depends on the temperature: 80° to 85°F. is ideal. The colder it is, the longer the batter should sit. Generally if it is ground in the morning, it should be ready for use by evening, except in winter when it will take at least 24 hours.

A chapati *tawa* or a heavy bottomed skillet should be used for making the dosas. Heat skillet and coat the bottom thinly with oil. The skillet should be neither too hot nor too cold. (To test the skillet, a drop of water should take a second to evaporate.) Ladle about half a cup of batter on middle of skillet and spread the batter around, making a fast, circular motion with the ladle. Movement should be done very deftly and quickly, before the batter hardens. Skill at this will come with practice. The batter should be spread thinly and evenly, like a French crepe. Sprinkle a few drops of oil over the dosa and allow it to cook for a minute or so. Using a wooden or steel spatula, gently lift the sides of the dosa, checking to see if it is firm. When it is firm, flip carefully. Dosas should have a golden color when cooked. This is a very popular South Indian dish and can be eaten with the Shyam *Sambar* (see p. 73) or any of the chutneys or sauces given in this book.

184. Bhaskara/Masala Dosas (Makes 20 to 25 Stuffed Dosas)

Make dosa batter given in preceding recipe.

Filling

5 large potatoes, boiled	1/2 cup shelled green peas
3 medium-sized carrots, coarsely grated	1/2 tsp. turmeric powder
1 onion, minced	salt to taste
2 tbs. minced coriander leaves	1/2 tsp. garam masala
1/2 cup oil	(see p. 23)

Heat 1 tablespoon of the oil in a frying pan and lightly sauté the onion. Then add the grated carrots, peas, turmeric, and salt and stir fry for 5 minutes. Skin and mash the potatoes lightly and add to the vegetable mixture. Stir well. Add garam masala and coriander leaves and mix thoroughly and set aside.

Heat a heavy-bottomed skillet and make the dosas according to the preceding recipe. Before flipping over with the spatula, spread 2 tablespoons of the filling on one half of each dosa. Fold the other half over the filling, so that it forms a semicircle. Then toast both sides for a few seconds. Remove from heat and serve; continue making dosas until batter is finished. Dosas are generally served immediately, straight from the skillet to the plate, otherwise they tend to become soggy. These masala dosas or stuffed pancakes may be eaten with either the Coconut Chutney or with the Shyam *Sambar*.

185. Balachandra/Utthappam or Indian Pizzas (Makes 20 to 25)
Make dosa batter according to recipe on page 109, except use about 3 tablespoons of water. (Batter should drop in lumps from ladle.)

5 medium-sized carrots, grated	1/2 cup oil
1 small cabbage, finely minced	salt and pepper to taste
2 large onion, finely minced	1/2 cup tomato sauce or
4 tbs. minced coriander leaves	1/2 cup tomato chutney

Add salt and pepper to taste to the thick dosa batter and mix well.

Heat a heavy-bottomed skillet and coat with a little of the oil. Fill a large ladle with the batter and spread it in the skillet to form a dosa about 1/4" thick and 6" in diameter. Sprinkle a few drops of oil over dosa. Immediately top it evenly with a tablespoon of the mixed vegetables. Lightly pat the vegetables with a spatula to embed them into the batter. Allow to cook for a minute or two until the underside is a golden brown. Gently flip to cook other side as well, then turn onto a plate. Dot with tomato sauce or tomato chutney and serve immediately. Continue until batter is finished. Should some batter be left over, it may be refrigerated and used the next day.

He who seeks to attain health by cheating Nature cheats only himself and, in consequence, suffers worse health.

—ACHARYA LAKSHMAN SHARMA

186. Vijaya/Ada or Spicy Dal Pancakes (Makes 15 to 20 Pancakes)

1 cup rice	1/4 cup chopped coriander leaves
1 cup mixed lentils (any kind)	1 large onion, minced
1/4 cup urad dal or black gram	1 tsp. black pepper powder
1 tsp. fenugreek seeds	1/4 cup oil
1/4 tsp. asafoetida	4 cups water
1 cup chopped spinach	salt to taste

Soak rice in 2 cups of water. Soak mixed lentils, black gram and fenugreek seeds in another 2 cups of water. Both should soak for a least 6 hours, or overnight. In the morning, wash, drain, and grind the rice and dals separately in a blender, then mix together. Batter should drop in lumps onto the skillet, as for *uttapams*.

To this batter, add the asafoetida, pepper, chopped greens, and salt and mix well. Heat a heavy-bottomed skillet and coat the bottom with a little oil. Fill a large ladle with the batter and spread it on the skillet to form a pancake about 1/4" thick and 6" in diameter.

Sprinkle a few drops of oil on top. Let it cook for about 2 minutes on one side. When it is firm, deftly turn it over and cook the other side. The color should be a golden brown when done. Serve hot with Coconut Chutney.

AUM TAT SAT

Everyone should discipline his tongue—overcome the sense of Taste— otherwise he will fall an easy prey to misery.

—Saint Thiruvalluvar

113

General Glossary

Aniseed *(saunf)*. This seed of the anise plant is an appetite stimulant and digestive that helps prevent flatulance. Aniseed is often served after meals.

Asafoetida *(hing)*. A pungent digestive gum resin with medicinal properties, asafoetida is frequently used in South Indian cooking.

Agar-Agar (China grass or seaweed). An extract of sea alga, agar is often used in puddings instead of gelatin.

Bay Leaf *(tej patta)*. An aromatic herb with preservative and germicidal properties, bay leaf is used fresh or dried for flavoring curries and other dishes.

Black Pepper *(kali mirch)*. Rich in vitamin C, black pepper is used to stimulate the heart and cure fevers and colds. It is said to be the first spice discovered by man. Obtained from the berries of the pepper vine, black pepper can be substituted for red chilies when a milder tasting dish is desired.

Cardamom *(ellaichi)*. This scented spice is used extensively in Indian cooking. Seed pods from the cardamom plant can be either large or small: the big black pods are used in curries and pulaus); the small green pods are used in sweet dishes.

Chilies, Red or Green *(mirch)*. Because they are so hot, dried red chilies are rarely used in the recipes in this book. Only the fresh tender green chilies, such as jalapeno or serrano, should be used and then *only after removing the seeds*, which are the hottest part. The skin contains vitamin C and lends a good flavor.

Cinnamon *(dalchini)*. Used in stick or powdered form in curries and sweets, cinnamon is a strong germicidal spice.

Cloves *(laung)*. These dried flower buds are used whole or in powdered form in sweets, curries, and garam masalas. Cloves are a powerful antiseptic.

Coriander *(dhania)*. The leaves of this herb, called cilantro, are a good source of vitamins; they are used extensively in recipes in this book for garnishing and flavoring. It is an aromatic herb, similar to parsley. Its seed form is a carminative. Coriander powder is used in many curries.

Cumin Seeds *(jeera)*. These seeds come from a plant belonging to the caraway family. Cumin seeds are either white or black; the white ones are more commonly used in Indian cooking. These seeds are also a digestive.

Curry Leaves *(meeta neem)*. Aromatic leaves used in South Indian curries and chutneys. Like bay leaves, they can be used dried or fresh and are digestive.

Fenugreek *(methi)*. The green leaves are rich in vitamin C and can be added to most vegetables. The seeds are rich in iron and can be used sparingly to flavor various dishes, since they are slightly bitter.

Ghee. Clarified butter.

Ginger *(adruk)*. This light brown, gnarled root is used in making curries and especially dals. It has medicinal properties and is a carminative. Ginger can also be dried and powdered and is used in sweets and cakes.

Jaggery. Unrefined cane sugar.

Jalapeno. See *Chilies*.

Legumes. Generic term for pod-bearing plants, like peas.

Mace *(javitri)*. Sold as blades or in powdered form, this spice is composed of the outer membrane of the nutmeg seed. It is used as a seasoning in curries and rice dishes.

Mango Powder *(amchoor)*. A tan-colored powder used in chutneys and curries instead of tamarind to impart a sour taste.

Mint *(podina)*. An aromatic herb used in chutneys and curries, mint is also good for herbal teas.

Mustard Seeds *(sarson ka beeja)*. These tiny yellow or black balls are rich in manganese and vitamin D. Pungent in flavor, they are used in most South Indian curries.

Nutmeg *(jaiphal)*. A digestive agent, nutmeg is used to flavor savories and puddings; it helps reduce flatulence.

Parsley *(ajmooda ka patta)*. Rich in Vitamin C and iron, parsley is used in salads and as a garnish.

Rose *(gulab)*. Both the red and pink variety have a good fragrance and can be used in making teas and flavoring certain types of puddings. Either fresh or dried leaves can be used.

Saffron *(kesar)*. The king of spices and perhaps the most expensive, saffron, with its delicate orange color, lends a unique flavor to pulaus and puddings. Saffron strands are the dried stigmata of the saffron plant, which grows in abundance in Kashmir. This spice has many medicinal properties.

Sesame Seeds *(til)*. These extremely nutritious seeds can be used as flavoring or made into butter.

Turmeric *(haldi)*. This root spice, which has a distinct yellow color, comes in powder form. It is widely used in many Indian dishes; it is also known for its antibacterial action.

116

Glossary of Hindi Terms

English	Hindi
Ash gourd	*Petta*
Bell Pepper	*Simla Mirch*
Beetroot	*Chukandar*
Bottle gourd	*Louki*
Eggplant	*Baingan*
Cabbage	*Bandhgobhi*
Carrot	*Gajar*
Cauliflower	*Gobhi*
Coriander	*Har dhania*
Cucumber	*Kheera (or Kakri)*
Green Beans	*Sem*
Fenugreek	*Methi*
Green Peas	*Matar*
Okra	*Bhindi*
Onions	*Pyaz*
Potato	*Aloo*
Pumpkin	*Kaddu*
White radish	*Mooli*
Snake gourd	*Chichinda*
Spinach	*Palak*
Scallion	*Hari pyaz*
Sweet corn	*Makkai*
Turnip	*Shalgam*
Tomato	*Tamatar*
Yam	*Suran*

	English	Hindi
Fruits	**English**	**Hindi**
	Apple	*Seb*
	Apricot	*Khumani*
	Banana	*Kela*
	Date	*Khejoor*
	Fig	*Angeer*
	Grapes	*Angoor*
	Guava	*Amrood*
	Lemon	*Gal-gal*
	Lime	*Nimbu*
	Mango	*Aam*
	Orange, Mandarin	*Santara*
	Sunkist	*Malta*
	Papaya	*Papita*
	Peach	*Aroo*
	Pear	*Naspati*
	Pineapple	*Ananas*
	Plum	*Ploom*
	Pomegranate	*Anar*
	Raisins	*Kishmish*
	Watermelon	*Tarbuz*
Nuts	Almonds	*Badaam*
	Cashew Nut	*Kaju*
	Coconut	*Nariyal*
	Peanut	*Moongfalli*
	Pistachio	*Pista*
	Walnut	*Akhroot*

English	Hindi	Cereals & Pulses
Barley	*Jawar*	
Split Chickpea	*Chana dal*	
Black garam	*Urad dal*	
Chickpea flour	*Besan*	
Corn	*Makkai*	
Cornflour	*Makkai ki atta*	
Red kidney beans	*Rajma*	
Dried chickpeas	*Kabuli chana*	
Dried split moong beans	*Moong dal*	
Lentil	*Masoor dal*	
Millet	*Bajra*	
Rice	*Chawal*	
Rice, long-grain	*Basmati*	
Semolina	*Sooji*	
Dried pigeon peas	*Toovar dal*	
Wheat	*Gehun*	
Whole wheat flour	*Atta*	
Whole green gram	*Sabat moong dal*	

The bodies of beings are born from food, food is produced from rain, rain comes from sacrifice, and sacrifice is born of action.

—BHAGAVAD GITA,
CHAPTER 3, VERSE 14

119

Glossary of Sanskrit Recipe Names

All recipes have been given Sanskrit names that have a special spiritual significance. The approximate meanings are given below. The meanings are listed in order of recipe number, not alphabetically. Chapter titles are in bold type.

Sadhana — Spiritual training and practice
1. *Archana* — Offering to God
2. *Pooja* — Ritualized form of worship
3. *Aradhana* — Worship and adoration of God
4. *Samyama* — Concentration and directing of the mind to achieve a yogic state
5. *Niyama* — Restraint of the mind
6. *Asana* — Yogic posture of the body
7. *Yoga* — Any activity leading to union with the Supreme
8. *Pranayama* — Yogic method of breath control
9. *Dharana* — Contemplation
10. *Japa* — Repetition of a mantra, mentally or on a rosary
11. *Dhyana* — Meditation
12. *Brahmacharya* — Sexual restraint and purity
13. *Dhriti* — Steadfastness in practicing sadhana
14. *Tapas* — Extreme austerity
15. *Samadhi* — Yogic trance

Gokul — Cowherd settlement where Krishna lived as a child
16. *Tulsi* — The holy basil plant, a favorite of Krishna's
17. *Abhaya* — Fearlessness
18. *Acharya* — Teacher
19. *Ahimsa* — Non-violence
20. *Akshara* — The immutable (quality of Brahman)

21. *Akasha*	Ether; subtlest of the five elements
22. *Ananda*	Bliss
23. *Avatara*	An incarnation of God
24. *Avikarya*	Devoid of all change (quality of Brahman)
25. *Avyakta*	Unmanifest (quality of Brahman)
26. *Atma*	The Self or embodied soul
Balakrishna	Krishna, as a baby
27. *Bhakti*	Devotion or love for God
28. *Bharta*	One who upholds (quality of the Supreme Lord)
29. *Bansali*	Krishna, the flute player
30. *Brindavan*	Forest where Krishna used to graze the cows as a child
31. *Brahman*	The formless Absolute
32. *Bhajan*	Devotional song
Damodara	Krishna, with a rope around his middle
33. *Deva*	A god
34. *Dharma*	The cosmic law of one's essential nature
35. *Advaita*	The philosophical doctrine of non-dualism
36. *Dhira*	Courageous
37. *Dwaraka*	The capital city of Krishna's state
38. *Devaki*	Krishna's mother
39. *Daruka*	Krishna's charioteer
40. *Draupadi*	Wife of Krishna's cousins, the Pandavas
41. *Vasudeva*	Krishna's father
42. *Yashoda*	Krishna's foster mother
43. *Nanda*	Krishna's foster father
44. *Subhadra*	Krishna's sister

45. *Kuchela*	Krishna's schoolmate
46. *Arjuna*	Krishna's great friend and cousin
47. *Yadava*	Krishna's clan
48. *Balarama*	Krishna's brother
Manamohan	Krishna, the stealer of the mind
49. *Radha*	Krishna's childhood sweetheart
50. *Rukmani*	Krishna's first wife
51. *Sathyabhama*	Krishna's wife
52. *Jambhavati*	Krishna's wife
53. *Mitrabinda*	Krishna's wife
54. *Sathya*	Krishna's wife
55. *Kalindi*	Krishna's wife
56. *Lakshmana*	Krishna's wife
57. *Bhadra*	Krishna's wife
Shyamasundara	Krishna, the beautiful black one
58. *Guru*	Spiritual teacher
59. *Gita*	Song; Short for Bhagavad Gita, the spiritual message given to Arjuna by Krishna
60. *Gopala*	Krishna, the cowherd boy
61. *Giridhara*	Krishna, the Lord of the cows
62. *Govinda*	Krishna, the uplifter of the mountain
63. *Gopi*	Cowherdess
64. *Hrishikesha*	The mountain that was lifted by Krishna
65. *Govardhan*	Krishna, the Lord of the senses
66. *Hari*	Name of Vishnu; Remover of sins
67. *Ishwara*	Lord; God
68. *Uddhava*	Friend of Lord Krishna
69. *Jeeva*	The individual soul

70. *Jnana*	Wisdom
71. *Jagadeeshwara*	Lord of the world

Krishna	Foremost avatar of Vishnu
72. *Keshava*	Krishna, the one with the luxurious hair
73. *Karma*	Actions that generate reactions
74. *Kama*	Desire
75. *Kausthubha*	The ruby worn by Vishnu
76. *Kaumodaki*	Lord Vishnu's mace
77. *Kanayya*	Krishna's name
78. *Mukunda*	Krishna, the giver of liberation
79. *Muraree*	Krishna, the killer of the demon Mura
80. *Madhava*	Vishnu, the consort of Lakshmi
81. *Moksha*	Spiritual liberation
82. *Mantra*	Sanskrit word charged with spiritual potency

Muralidhar	Krishna, the holder of the flute
83. *Mitra*	Name of the sun God
84. *Murali*	Flute
85. *Madhusudhan*	Vishnu, the killer of the demon Madhu
86. *Madana*	Krishna, the intoxicating one
87. *Manohar*	Krishna, the one who steals the mind
88. *Madhuvan*	A forest where Krishna used to tend the cows
89. *Maharishi*	Great sage

Chaitanya	Divine consciousness
90. *Muni*	Sage or hermit
91. *Maya*	The illusory power of the Lord
92. *Nishkama*	Free from desire
93. *Nirmala*	Free from impurities

94. *Naivedya*	Offering of food to God
Narayana	Vishnu, the one who lies on the cosmic waters
95. *Paramatma*	The supreme soul
96. *Pundareekaksha*	Vishnu, the lotus-eyed one
97. *Pushpanjali*	An offering of flowers to God
98. *Parthasarathi*	Krishna, the driver of Arjuna's chariot
99. *Padmanabha*	Vishnu, from whose navel sprang the world lotus
100. *Pavithra*	Immaculate
101. *Purusha*	The primeval person
102. *Prakriti*	The Nature of the active priniciple of Purusha
103. *Rishi*	Seer or sage
104. *Parikshit*	Grandson of Arjuna and Krishna's grand-nephew
105. *Arati*	Offering of light and camphor before the deity
106. *Pradyumna*	Krishna's son by Rukmani
107. *Anirudha*	Pradyumna's son and Krishna's grandson
108. *Divya*	Divine
109. *Aryan*	Scion of the Aryan race
110. *Bhagavan*	Possessor of the eight-fold qualities of Lordship
111. *Nirguna*	Without qualities (quality of Brahman)
112. *Yogeeshwara*	Greatest of yogis
113. *Homa*	A ritual fire sacrifice
Nandakumar	Krishna, son of Nanda
114. *Shyam*	Krishna, the dark one
115. *Sannyas*	Renunciation of worldly ties
116. *Tyagi*	One who renounces
117. *Kalyan*	Good fortune

118. *Mangala*	Auspiciousness
119. *Sadharmya*	Becoming one with the law of divine Being
120. *Salokya*	Dwelling with the divine
121. *Samata*	Equality of mind with all beings
122. *Sattva*	Having the quality of purity and divinity
123. *Sathya*	Truth
124. *Shakti*	The divine energy
125. *Shastra*	The holy scriptures
126. *Sadhu*	A holy man
127. *Siddhi*	Supernormal power
128. *Shraddha*	Faith
129. *Swadharma*	Personal law of action
130. *Sudarshan*	Name of Lord Vishnu's discus
131. *Sampoorna*	Eternally full (quality of Brahman)
132. *Shanti*	Peace
133. *Samba*	Krishna's son by Jambhavathi
134. *Samarpan*	To dedicate to God
135. *Sadhaka*	One who does sadhana
136. *Shree*	The consort of Lord Vishnu
137. *Sharanam*	Refuge or recourse (pertaining to God)

Vishveshwara	Lord of the Universe
138. *Tejas*	Brilliance of physical energy
139. *Ojas*	Brilliance of spiritual energy
140. *Ananta*	Serpent couch of Lord Vishnu
141. *Turiya*	The fourth state of consciousness
142. *Tapovan*	Forest of austerity
143. *Anaadi*	Beginningless (quality of Brahman)
144. *Uttama*	Highest
145. *Vairagya*	Detachment

146. *Vedanta*	Last portion of the Vedas
147. *Veda*	The ancient Hindu scriptures
148. *Vibhuti*	Special manifestation of divine power or glory
149. *Viveka*	Discrimination between Real and Unreal
150. *Yajna*	A special sacrifice to the gods
151. *Yuga*	An age or vast cycle of time
152. *Nirvana*	Supreme peace
153. *Brahmin*	A member of the priestly class
Poornanand	Full of bliss
154. *Krishnamrit*	The nectar of Krishna
155. *Krishnanand*	Krishna's delight
156. *Aja*	Unborn (quality of Brahman)
157. *Aishwarya*	Material wealth supported by spiritual wealth
158. *Achintya*	Beyond thought (quality of Brahman)
159. *Sanathana*	Ancient (pertaining to Hindu religion)
160. *Krishnapriya*	Beloved of Krishna
161. *Vaikund*	Abode of Lord Vishnu
162. *Vyasa*	The sage who authored the Mahabharatha and all the puranas
163. *Surya Narayana*	The divine in the form of the sun
164. *Swami*	Lord, master, or Holy one
165. *Shauri*	Krishna, the head of the Shoora clan
166. *Upanishad*	The last portion of the Vedas
167. *Ramana*	The one who delights
168. *Mahalakshmi*	Consort of Lord Vishnu
169. *Jagannath*	Master of the world
170. *Shriniketan*	The abode of auspiciousness
171. *Keertan*	Devotional song

172. *Deenadayal*	He who is compassionate to the afflicted (quality of Ishwara)
173. *Shreekhand*	The source of auspiciousness
Vanamali	Krishna, the wearer of a garland of wild flowers
174. *Amala*	Pure
175. *Janardan*	Krishna, the one who destroys the pangs of birth and death
176. *Leela*	The cosmic play
177. *Mohan*	Krishna, the enticer
178. *Devadas*	The servant of God
179. *Achyutha*	Name of Vishnu, meaning the unshakeable one
180. *Nitya*	Eternal (quality of Brahman)
181. *Poorna*	Completely fulfilled (quality of Brahman)
182. *Devi*	Goddess
183. *Rama*	Incarnation of Lord Vishnu
184. *Bhaskara*	The sun God
185. *Balachandra*	The new (baby) moon
186. *Vijaya*	Victory

Fasting, water, sun, air, and right diet cure all the ills and keep the mind quiet.

—Kavi Yogi Maharshi
Shuddhananda Bharatiar

With these two hundred names, we worship thee, O Vanamali.
A garland of wild flowers at Thy Lotus Feet.

HARI OM TAT SAT

Index